"This study of *Hamlet* is a kind of thrill ride, a breathless investigation of some of the most important ideas from philosophy and psychoanalysis from the Modern era."
    —Charles Baxter, author of *The Feast of Love*

"Brilliant. . . . *Hamlet* is, as everyone knows, about everything, but it's also about nothing, or rather, nothingness. . . . *Stay, Illusion!* penetrates to the center of this paradox. A thrilling performance."
    —David Shields, author of *Reality Hunger*

"A hugely enjoyable, aphoristic, punky, intellectually dazzling bomb of a book: a serious provocation to both the biscuit-box Shakespeare industry and, more widely, to contemporary literary culture. . . . [*Stay, Illusion!*] is a book to be devoured, argued with, spat out."   —*The Independent* (London)

"Critchley and Webster write about *Hamlet* in short, vitriolic chapters, proposing a series of darkly intelligent questions. . . . It is an ode to the spirit of 'rashness.'"   —*New Statesman*

"Insightful. . . . The authors' passion for the play and its questions are clearly evident."
    —*Publishers Weekly*

"Lively and thoughtful. . . . Erudite, witty and probing, *Stay, Illusion!* offers new insights into a literary touchstone while deepening our appreciation for its complexity and its enigmatic core."
    —*Shelf Awareness*

SIMON CRITCHLEY & JAMIESON WEBSTER

Stay, Illusion!

Simon Critchley is Hans Jonas Professor of Philosophy at the New School for Social Research. His many books include *Very Little . . . Almost Nothing*, *The Faith of the Faithless*, and *The Book of Dead Philosophers*. He is the series moderator of The Stone, a philosophy column in *The New York Times*, to which he is a frequent contributor.

Jamieson Webster is a psychoanalyst in private practice in New York City. She is the author of *The Life and Death of Psychoanalysis* and has written for *The Aesthete*, *Apology*, *Cabinet*, *The Guardian*, *The Huffington Post*, *Playboy*, *The New York Times*, and many psychoanalytic publications. She teaches at Eugene Lang College at the New School and supervises doctoral students in clinical psychology at the City University of New York.

Stay, Illusion!

Stay, Illusion!

THE HAMLET DOCTRINE

Simon Critchley

&

Jamieson Webster

VINTAGE BOOKS

A DIVISION OF RANDOM HOUSE LLC

NEW YORK

FIRST VINTAGE BOOKS EDITION, APRIL 2014

Copyright © 2013 by Simon Critchley and Jamieson Webster

The Library of Congress has cataloged the Pantheon edition as follows:
Critchley, Simon.
Stay, illusion! : the Hamlet doctrine /
Simon Critchley and Jamieson Webster.
p. cm.
Includes bibliographical references and index.
1. Shakespeare, William, 1564–1616—Hamlet. 2. Shakespeare,
William, 1564–1616—Influence. 3. Hamlet (Legendary character).
I. Webster, Jamieson. II. Title.
PR2807.C74 2013   822.3'3—dc23   2012039269

Vintage Trade Paperback ISBN: 978-0-307-95048-2
eBook ISBN: 978-0-307-90762-2

Author photograph © Isabel Asha Penzlien
Book design by Robert C. Olsson

www.vintagebooks.com

For Soren

Moreover, it is time in any case to oppose this mendacious world with the resources of an irony, a shrewdness, a serenity without illusions. For, supposing we were to lose, we would be able to lose cheerfully, without condemning, without prophesying. We are not looking for a rest. If the world insists on blowing up, we may be the only ones to grant it a right to do so, while giving ourselves the right to have spoken in vain.

—Georges Bataille

CONTENTS

PART III

CONCLUSION

Introduction

Praised Be Rashness

THIS LITTLE BOOK is the late-flowering fruit of a shared obsession. Although Hamlet makes himself crystal clear during his lambasting of Ophelia, "I say, we will have no mo marriage," we are married, and Shakespeare's play, its interpretation, and philosophical interpreters have been a goodly share of our connubial back and forth over the last couple of years. We are outsiders to the world of Shakespeare criticism and have chosen as a way into the play a series of outsider interpretations of *Hamlet,* notably those of Carl Schmitt, Walter Benjamin, Hegel, Freud, Lacan, and Nietzsche. What each of these interpretations enables is a bold but sometimes distant and *rash* take on *Hamlet.* We will try to use these interpretations as a set of levers with which to twist open a closer and, we hope, compelling textual engagement with the play itself. Not that we are above rashness ourselves, and if an approach shapes our interpretation, that we might dupe the reader by calling a methodology, then it takes its cue from Virginia Woolf. In her wonderful essay "On Being Ill," she writes:

> Rashness is one of the properties of illness—outlaws that we are—and it is rashness that we need in reading Shakespeare. It is not that we should doze in reading him, but that, fully conscious and aware, his fame intimidates and bores, and all the views of all

the critics dull in us that thunder clap of conviction which, if an illusion, is still so helpful an illusion, so prodigious a pleasure, so keen a stimulus in
reading the great. Shakespeare is getting flyblown;
a paternal government might well forbid writing
about him, as they put his monument at Stratford
beyond the reach of scribbling fingers. With all this
buzz of criticism about, one may hazard one's conjectures privately, making one's notes in the margin;
but, knowing that someone has said it before, or
said it better, the zest is gone. Illness, in its kingly
sublimity, sweeps all that aside and leaves nothing
but Shakespeare and oneself. What with his overweening power and our overweening arrogance, the
barriers go down, the knots run smooth, the brain
rings and resounds with *Lear* or *Macbeth,* and even
Coleridge himself squeaks like a distant mouse.

In the name of zest, and in order to make brains ring and
Shakespeare resound, we will proceed, as Hamlet says
to Horatio, "Rashly—And praised be rashness for it."

The Gap Between Thought and Action

FOR SOME, and it is a popular view that goes back at least to Goethe, Hamlet is a man who simply cannot make up his mind: he waits, hesitates, and is divided from himself in his "madness," all the while dreaming of a redeeming, cataclysmic violence. In this view, Hamlet is a creature of endless vacillation, a cipher for the alienated inward modern self in a world that is insubstantial and rotten: "Denmark's a prison," Hamlet sighs. For others, Hamlet is the great melancholic who is jealous of Claudius because he has realized his secret desire, namely, to usurp the place of his rival in the affection of his mother.

For still others, Hamlet is not so much a bather in the black sun of depression as too much in the sun of knowledge. Through the medium of the ghost, he has grasped the nature of that which is; that is, himself, his family, and the corrupt political order that surrounds him. Unlike some of the heroes in Attic tragedy, like Oedipus, who act first and then find out the truth later, Hamlet knows the truth from the ghost's mouth in act I. This truth does not lead to action but instead to a disgust with or nausea from existence. In this view, Hamlet is a kind of anti-Oedipus: whereas the latter moves ragefully from ignorance to knowledge, and his insight requires the loss of his sight in a violent act of self-blinding, the great Dane knows the score from the get-go, but such knowledge does not seem to lead to action. Maybe action requires veils of illusion, and once those veils are lifted, we feel a sense of resignation.

Whatever the truth of the various interpretations, there seems to be a significant disconnection between thought and action in the person of Hamlet. Consider the famous "To be, or not to be" soliloquy. After contemplating suicide as an attempted "quietus" from a "weary life," Hamlet ponders the dread of life after death, "the undiscovered country from whose bourn no traveler returns" (apart from the ghost, of course, who seems to have a return ticket). The possibility of life after death "puzzles the will" and makes us endure the sufferings that we have rather than risk ones we know nothing of but that could be much worse. He continues:

> Thus conscience does make cowards of us all,
> And thus the native hue of resolution
> Is sicklied over with the pale cast of thought,
> And enterprises of great pitch and moment,
> With this regard their currents turn awry
> And lose the name of action.

Thought and action seem to pull against each other, the former annulling the possibility of the latter. If, as Hamlet says elsewhere, "there is nothing either good or bad but thinking makes it so," then thinking makes things rather bad, and any resolution dissolves into thin air. Speaking of thin air, we might notice that when the ghost makes his final appearance in the play, in a scene of almost-unbearable verbal and near-physical violence, with Hamlet raging at his mother for her inconstancy, the ghost says that "This visitation / is but to whet thy almost blunted purpose." Hamlet confesses to being a "tardy son" who has not committed "Th' important acting" of the ghost's command.

The ghost asks Hamlet to step between his mother and her fighting soul and speak the truth. For a moment it seems as if he might—"dear mother, you are sleeping with your husband's murderer." But as she mumbles the word "ecstasy," Hamlet careens into the most pathetic of adjurations, begging Gertrude not to sleep again with Claudius, laying down arms before the truth, once again. "Conceit in weakest bodies strongest works," the ghost says.

The Mouse-trap

THE ONLY WAY in which it appears that Hamlet can attempt to close the gap between thought and action is through the ultimate conceit, that is, through *theater,* through play. The purpose of the play within the play in act 3, *The Mouse-trap,* is to produce a thing that will catch the conscience of the king. But as Hamlet is acutely aware—and, one naïvely presumes, that enigma that we name "Shakespeare" who lurks ghostly in the wings (and there is an ancient, if unverifiable, tradition that Shakespeare played the role of the ghost in the original performance, opposite Richard Burbage's Hamlet)—a play is nothing, namely, nothing real. It is, rather, "a fiction . . . a dream of passion" and this realization is somehow "monstrous." Theater is "all for nothing." What are the sufferings of Hecuba or indeed Hamlet to us? Yet, Hamlet would seem to be suggesting that the manifest fiction of theater is the only vehicle in which the truth might be presented.

The trap works, and the mouse-king's conscience is caught. The dumb show reenactment of Hamlet Senior's murder pricks the king's conscience, and he flees the theater calling for "light." We then find Claudius alone confessing his fratricidal crime, "O, my offense is rank." On the way to his mother's bedroom, to which he's been summoned, Hamlet passes Claudius kneeling in futile prayer. With Claudius genuflecting, head bowed, it is clear that *now* Hamlet could do it. With one swoop of his sword, thought and action would be reconciled and Hamlet's father revenged. But at that precise moment, Hamlet begins to *think* and decides that this is the wrong moment to kill Claudius because he is at prayer and trying to make his amends with heaven. It is "hire and salary," he says, "not revenge." Hamlet then fantasizes about killing Claudius at the right moment, "When he is drunk asleep, or in his rage, or in th' incestuous pleasure of his bed." He sheathes his sword and moves quickly to meet Gertrude, repeatedly and manically calling her: "Mother, mother, mother!" Following the express instructions of the ghost, Hamlet has resolved to use no more in his encounter with his mother than words, words, words: "I will speak daggers to her, but use none."

It is not that Hamlet *cannot* act. He kills Polonius, sends Rosencrantz and Guildenstern to their doom in England, is quasi-responsible for the death of Ophelia, and eventually dispatches Claudius. But the death of Polonius is inadvert; he hears a noise from behind the arras and suddenly strikes and then insouciantly asks, "Is it the king?" having just left Claudius alive seconds earlier. Rosencrantz and Guildenstern die in his stead offstage—a complex letter-exchanging act of self-preservation involving piracy and ship switching that even impressed Freud, given Hamlet's otherwise morbid inhibition. Poor Ophelia's suicide is something like a tragic casualty of Hamlet's unrelenting cruelty toward her. Killing Polonius is the coup de grâce in Ophelia's unfolding psychosis. And the intended victim, Claudius, is only murdered when Hamlet has been hit with the poisoned rapier and knows that he is going to die: "I am dead, Horatio," Hamlet repeats in three variations in a little more than twenty lines. The dying Laertes spills the beans about the plot with the poisoned rapiers and wine, "the king's to blame," and Hamlet stabs Claudius to death after just one line's reflection: "The point envenomed too? / Then venom do thy work!"

Let Be

If thought kills action, then action must be thoughtless—
such would appear to be Hamlet's credo. The cost of
the infinite self-reflexivity of which Hamlet is capable
is incapacity of action. Such, one might ponder, is the
curse of self-consciousness, which gives us extraordinary
insight into ourselves but whose boon companions are
melancholy, alienation, and a massive obstruction at
the level of action. Inhibition hems Hamlet in. Another
consequence: after the savage dissolution of Ophelia as
his object of love, there is little left to Hamlet of eros.
If hell, as Dostoevsky says, is the inability to love, then
Hamlet's selfhood is infernal.

Is that it? Are we left with the unanswerable onto-
logical question "To be, or not to be?"—with the strong
sense that Hamlet's preference is for the negative clause
after the comma? Or "if philosophy could find it out,"
might there not be another moral to draw from the
play?

A different line of thought is suggested by the deeply
enigmatic speech given to the ever-trusty Horatio just
before Hamlet is about to fight with Laertes in a conflict that he intuits will cost him his life.

> We defy augury. There is special providence in the
> fall of a sparrow. If it be now, 'tis not to come; if it
> be not to come, it will be now; if it be not now, yet it

will come. The readiness is all. Since man, of aught
he leaves, knows aught, what is't to leave betimes?
Let be.

Generations of readers have interpreted these lines in
relation to the Christian idea of Providence and linked
them to Hamlet's earlier words, "There is a divinity
that shapes our ends." This might be correct, but perhaps these words can withstand another, slightly more
skeptical, gloss.

The words "Let be" might be heard as a response to
the question "To be, or not to be?" But what might that
mean? It is the defiance of augury that is most interesting in the preceding passage, the refusal of any ability
on our part to predict the future, to claim the power
to foresee the course of events. But if that is true, then
the second verse might be intended slightly ironically:
that is, "What, you mean, there's a special providence
in the fall of a sparrow?" The point might be that if
there is any providence at work, then we know nothing of it. Such knowledge is the unique attribute of
the divinity of whom we mere mortals can know nothing, rough-hew his/her/its ends how we will. Knowing
nothing, letting be, mean for Hamlet that "the readiness is all." Is this, then, how we might understand the
knot of negations that crowd the next lines of the text?
If it be now, then it is not come, and if it is to come,
then it is not now. The wisdom here seems close to
Epicurus: When death is, I am not; when I am, death
is not; therefore why worry?

Bunghole

PERHAPS THE GAP between thought and action can never be bridged. And perhaps this is the skeptical lesson of *Hamlet* for modern philosophy and modern readers. But such skepticism is not a reason for either depression or the "antic disposition" of seeming madness: Hamlet's endlessly oscillating mood swings between melancholia and mania. It might allow for something else, for example, the rather-grim humor that punctuates *Hamlet*. Think of the Danish punster's endless wordplays. Hamlet's first words in the play, in response to Claudius addressing him as his son, are a pun—"A little more than kin, and less than kind"—so it goes on for much of the ensuing action. Think also of the extraordinary scene between Hamlet and the clown who also doubles as a gravedigger (good comedians always know where the bodies are buried). Everyone knows the "Alas, poor Yorick" speech, but what is less well known is the way in which Alexander the Great becomes the bunghole in a beer barrel. Hamlet provides the precise reasoning:

> Alexander died, Alexander was buried, Alexander returneth into dust, the dust is earth, of earth we make loam and why of that loam, whereto he was converted, might they not stop a beer-barrel?

But wait, it gets weirder. Warming to his morbid theme, Hamlet delivers a quatrain:

Imperious Caesar, dead and turned to clay,
Might stop a hole to keep the wind away:
O, that that earth which kept the world in awe,
Should patch a wall to expel the winter's flaw!

With admirable anal imagery, Alexander the bung-hole becomes Caesar the wind stop. If we are good for little else than stopping up holes, if we are Hamlet-like creatures, divided against ourselves between thought and action, then perhaps this division can be borne by humor, indeed a rather-noir comic realism.

The readiness is all, provided we can cultivate a disposition of skeptical openness that does not claim to know aught of what we truly know naught. If we can cure ourselves of our longing for some sort of god-like conspectus of what it means to be human, or the construction of ourselves as some new prosthetic God through technology, bound by the self-satisfied myth of unlimited human progress, then we might *let be.* This, we would insist, is why we need theater, especially tragedy—"absent thee from felicity awhile."

In Hamlet's final words, "The rest is silence."

The Gorgiastic Paradox of Theater

FROM THE VERY BEGINNING, with the arguments of books 2, 3, and 10 of Plato's *Republic,* philosophy has had a huge problem with theater. It is no exaggeration to say that philosophy begins *as* a problem with theater. In order to be able to imagine a legitimate political regime orientated toward truth, Socrates claims that it is necessary to exclude theater in general and the tragic poets in particular. For theater is not concerned with truth. It is entirely preoccupied with the production of *deception,* with illusion and fakery. For Plato, democracy (*demokratia*) is what he calls in *Laws,* a *theatrokratia,* a theatrocracy, where political power passes through theatrical display. In other words, democracy is a society of the spectacle that legitimates itself through the production of theatrical or mediatic illusion that gives the impression of legitimacy without any genuine substance. Against the deception of *demokratia,* which leads only to tyranny in Plato's view—which is why tyrants are so fond of theater—he posits *philosophia,* a new regime in both the city and the soul based on justice and directed toward the good. But Plato is canny enough to know that, in order to be persuasive, the philosophical lawgivers must conceive of themselves as rival poets. Philosophy therefore has to displace theater with a drama of its own. This is what finds expression in the elaborate fictional conceit of the Socratic dialogues. Plato's stroke of theatrical genius was to replace the tragic sufferings of Oedipus, Ajax, or whoever with another, loftier heroic ideal: the dying Socrates. Tragedy comes off the stage only to enter the drama of public life.

To get a clearer idea of what worried Plato so much about theater, and tragedy in particular, consider the following fragment from Gorgias, the highly influential Sicilian rhetorician and sophist who introduced much of the teaching of oratory to Athens in the latter half of the fifth century BCE. Socrates targets Gorgias implicitly in the *Republic* and explicitly in the dialogue that bears his name. This fragment is fascinating, however, because—along with Aristophanes's *The Frogs*—it gives us our earliest extant "theoretical" response to ancient tragedy. As is well known, the ancient Greek word for "theory" (*theoria*) is linked to *theoros,* the spectator in a theater, and can be connected to the verb that denotes the act of seeing or contemplation (*theorein*). If Aristotle was right to say that tragedy is an imitation of action, *mimesis praxeos*—for it is the realm of action that will decide whether human beings are happy or unhappy—then action or praxis is always viewed from a theoretical standpoint. Theater is always theoretical, and theory is a theater, where we are spectators of a drama that unfolds: *our* drama. Yet, this drama is a deception. Gorgias writes:

> Tragedy, by means of legends and emotions, creates a deception in which the deceiver is more honest than the non-deceiver and the deceived is wiser than the non-deceived.

The Greek noun whose various declensions and negations is doing all the work in this fragment is *apate,* which Liddell and Scott's Greek lexicon tells us means "cheating, trickery, fraud, guile, deceit, and cunning." It also connotes a stratagem in war. Altogether, it's a pretty bad thing.

But consider the logic of the fragment: tragedy is a deception or an act of fraud or trickery, in which the deceiver is more honest than the nondeceiver, and the deceived is wiser than the nondeceived. What Gorgias seems to describe—perhaps even celebrate—is precisely that which Plato sees as the great danger of tragedy, the danger of deception that leads to a *theatrocratic* political regime based on nothing more than the affective effects of imitation and illusion.

The vast question that Gorgias's fragment raises is that of the necessity—and indeed the moral and political productivity—of deception, of fiction, of fraud, of illusion. Is the truth best said or perhaps only said in a fiction; that is, in a lie and a falsehood? Might not the dubious legends of tragedy and the fake emotions they induce leave the deceived spectator in the theater wiser and more honest than the undeceived philosopher who wants to do away with *theatrocracy*? But is this not also monstrous?

Ass, Ho, Hum

HAMLET GRASPS the founding Gorgiastic paradox of theater with extraordinary clarity and conceptual precision, and it horrifies him. Having been confronted with the truth of his father's murder by the ghost in act 1, Hamlet drifts distracted, melancholic, and "mad" in the early scenes of act 2 until the appearance of the players and the germ of the idea of the play within the play. Hamlet recalls a trip to the theater, although it is hardly clear where this is meant to have taken place: Elsinore? Wittenberg? London? Indeed, Hamlet seems to know the players rather well, "Dost thou hear me, old friend," he says to the first player. Hamlet begins to cite from memory a speech from a production of the tale of Aeneas and Dido that is then picked up and ventriloquized by the first player. It deals with the slaughter of Priam and, more particularly, the reaction of Hecuba, "the mobled queen," to her husband's murder by Pyrrhus. The moral purpose of the theatrical memory is clear: Gertrude is no mobled queen. Hecuba was a genuinely mournful wife whose "burst of clamor" would have made the gods weep with its passion. At this point, the ever-idiotic Polonius, the daddy of all windbags, asks the player to stop and says, "Look, whe'r he has not turned his color, and has tears in's eyes." The Gorgiastic deceptive power of theater is clear for all to see. Actors can even weep real tears, "either for tragedy, comedy, history, pastoral, pastoral-comical, historical-pastoral, tragical-historical, tragical comical-historical-pastoral, scene individable, or poem unlimited."

Hamlet then hastily arranges the production of "The Murder of Gonzago" for the following day and quickly dismisses the players, along with Polonius, Rosencrantz, and Guildenstern. The stage empty—while still, of course, visible onstage and we can eavesdrop—Hamlet turns suddenly inward:

> Now I am alone.
> O, what a rogue and peasant slave am I!
> Is it not monstrous that this player here,
> But in a fiction, in a dream of passion,
> Could force his soul so to his own conceit
> That from her working all his visage wanned,
> Tears in his eyes, distraction in's aspéct,
> A broken voice, and his whole function suiting
> With forms to his conceit? And all for nothing!
> For Hecuba!
> What's Hecuba to him or he to Hecuba,
> That he should weep for her?

Hamlet understands the logic of Gorgias's provocation and is appalled. How can a historical nothing, a zero, like the fate of the destitute and destroyed Trojan queen, move us? In what does the power of such a fiction, such a conceit, such a dream of passion, consist? Hamlet here objects to the basic conceit of theater in almost Platonic terms. If this player can weep for a theatrical aberration from the dim and distant Mycenaean past, like Hecuba, then, Hamlet goes on:

> What would he do,
> Had he the motive and cue for passion

That I have? He would drown the stage with
tears . . .

If Hamlet were an actor, or, better, the first player
played Hamlet—and notice the amazing reflexivity of
the drama upon drama that we are seeing onstage as a
drama here—then the truth that the ghost reveals to
Hamlet would "Confound the ignorant, and amaze
indeed / The very faculties of eyes and ears." If Hamlet
was an actor in a tragedy called *Hamlet,* then this would
put the sufferings of Hecuba into the shade, and we
would see the deception of theater in its true light, in
the light of the truth. Some interpreters—indeed one
we will meet quite soon—would argue that, because
of its relative historical proximity at the beginning of
our alleged "modernity," the tragedy of Hamlet does
indeed put that of Hecuba and the other heroes and
heroines of antiquity into the shadows. (The most cur-
sory reading of Euripides's *Hecuba,* the most Beckettian
and tragic-comic of ancient dramas, would explode this
modern prejudice.)

Yet, the problem here—and it is a mighty caveat—is
that Hamlet cannot speak the truth. He wheels round
violently upon himself:

> Yet I,
> A dull and muddy-mettled rascal, peak
> Like John-a-dreams, unpregnant of my cause,
> And can say nothing.

We will come back to this word "nothing," which
peppers, punctuates, and seems to structure the entire
action of *Hamlet* and what we might see as its nihilism. But the point that Hamlet is making is that if
anyone had true cause for justified action, then it is
he. Yet he can do nothing, say nothing. He is para-

lyzed with a secret whose truth he cannot divulge. The play called *The Tragicall Historie of Hamlet, Prince of Denmarke* should, in truth, be the greatest of dramas, but it is doomed to fail because that truth cannot be spoken. Hamlet then suddenly imagines being called a villain and a coward and—like a true actor—feigns indignation: "Who calls me villain?" But then begins the most remorseless series of self-accusations and self-lacerations:

> I am pigeon-livered and lack gall . . .
> Bloody, bawdy villain!
> Remorseless, treacherous, lecherous, kindless villain!
> O vengeance!
> Why, what an ass am I?

After turning on himself—ass first, as it were—Hamlet then turns upon language itself. Because he cannot take revenge against Claudius, he avenges himself on the very words of the soliloquy that he is speaking. Hamlet is the son of a murdered father whose purgatorially confinèd ghost has told the truth. Yet Hamlet cannot speak it or act on it. On the contrary:

> I . . . Must like a whore unpack my heart with words,
> And fall a-cursing like a very drab,
> A scullion!

Self-abhorred, Hamlet compares himself to a whore. The word and its many cognates—"drab," "scullion," "bawd"—abound around the play. Now, in the opening lines of *Rameau's Nephew*, Diderot famously compares his thoughts to whores (*Mes pensées, ce sont mes catins*). Yet, if this comparison is done in the spirit of a certain Epicurean libertinage, then Hamlet's words are simply pebbles that rattle the bars of language's prison house or, rather, the brothel of fake emotion within which he finds himself confined through his cowardice.

Next, a strange thing happens: having passed through "ass," we shift from a "ho" to "hum." Hamlet turns himself around once again with an uncanny imperative: "About, my brains!" There then follows a single-word line, a pause or even caesura in the lava flow of self-loathing:

Hum.

This simple "hum," which is repeated in act 5, leads Hamlet to back away from the truth—that he cannot act and unpacks his cowardly heart with words like a mere drab or scullion—and back toward Gorgias's economy of theatrical deception. His mood suddenly shifted, Hamlet says to himself:

I have heard that guilty creatures sitting at a play
Have by the very cunning of the scene
Been struck to the soul that presently
They have proclaimed their malefactions.

Of course, the thought here is that the play's the thing wherein to catch the conscience of the king. So, having lambasted the fake pretense of theater— most Plato-like—barely a minute earlier, Hamlet now embraces it with the reasoning that somehow the fakery of the play will awaken the king's conscience, and he will confess his crime. If theater is good for nothing, then perhaps it will be good for this nothing—the unspoken crime of a "king of shreds and patches"—that must be brought out into the open.

As Hamlet ponders the possibility of eliciting a confession, he suddenly introduces a new and bewildering secondary argument. He begins to *doubt* the ghost:

The spirit that I have seen
May be a devil, and the devil hath power
T'assume pleasing shape.

Perhaps the ghost was no ghost. Perhaps its truth, like theater itself, was a lie. Perhaps the apparition of the dead father was a devilish deceit, jiggery-pokery, or even popery. In which case, Hamlet cannot trust the ghost's evidence and requires, like a California lawyer, secondary and independent proof of Claudius's guilt through a confession. But if Hamlet believes that, then perhaps he is a coward and a whore after all.

We move from one meaning of the turning of tricks to another. The threshold between truth and doubt cannot be established. Hamlet, with the introduction of even a single doubt, will begin to doubt everything, like Descartes in his Dutch oven. The dike of truth is breached by a flood of doubt. Hamlet is left stranded on the shores of a world-cum-brothel whose prime instigator is theater herself. We are reminded of Freud's comments at the end of *Notes upon a Case of Obsessional Neurosis:*

> The doubt corresponds to the patient's internal perception of his own indecision, which, in consequence of the inhibition of his love by his hatred, takes possession of him in the face of every intended action. The doubt is in reality a doubt of his own love—which ought to be the most certain thing in his mind; and it becomes diffused over everything else, and is especially apt to become displaced on to what is most insignificant and small. A man who doubts his own love may, or rather *must,* doubt every lesser thing.[1]

At the end of this passage Freud footnotes the love verses written by Hamlet to Ophelia, spoken by Polonius to the king and queen:

Doubt thou the stars are fire;
Doubt that the sun doth move;
Doubt truth to be a liar;
But never doubt I love.

We are, and Freud is well aware of this, an earshot away from the scene where Hamlet—with these love verses returned to him—accuses Ophelia of being nothing but a whore, a would-be breeder of sinners. "You should not have believed me," he says to Ophelia; she should have doubted his love, as he does, along with everything else.

To recapitulate the rather-odd sequence of Hamlet's claims, which—it must not be forgotten—are made onstage, in a theater, in a necessarily deceptive tragedy:

1. Theater is a powerful but monstrous fiction that produces fake emotion and adds up to nothing.
2. Compared with the fakery of the tragedy of Hecuba recounted by the first player, *The Tragicall Historie of Hamlet, Prince of Denmarke,* whose core would be the truth spoken by the ghost, would be a real drama that, if acted, would, "Make mad the guilty and appal the free."
3. Yet this truth cannot be spoken or acted upon, and Hamlet declares himself an ass, a coward, and a whore.
4. Nonetheless, Hamlet says he has heard that theater can move criminals to confess their crimes. Therefore, he will order the players to play something like his father's murder in the slaying of Gonzago.
5. Furthermore, this play within a play is necessary because it will provide secondary confirmation

of the ghost's claims, for maybe the "Truepenny"
ghost was a lying, counterfeit devil.

6. Perhaps, Hamlet avers, the truth at the heart of
Hamlet is no truth at all, which seems equivalent to
the thought that Hamlet has no heart as a result of
self-doubt, stranding him on the shores of nihilism.

It Nothing Must

Is HAMLET A nihilist drama? Is it really a play about nothing? We kept noticing occurrences of the word "nothing" in *Hamlet* and then began to link them together and discovered that nothing, as it were, structures the action of the play and the interplay between its central characters. In a deep sense, this is indeed a play about nothing. We'd like to enumerate these nothings and then, like T. S. Eliot on Margate Sands recovering from a nervous breakdown, see if we can connect nothing with nothing. In the enigmatic words of the player queen in *The Mouse-trap:* "it nothing must."

THE GHOST

In the opening lines of the play, Marcellus asks Barnardo if the ghost, "this thing," has appeared again, and he replies, "I have seen nothing." The ghost *is* nothing, of course, so Barnardo confesses that he has seen it, that is, not seen it. In matters ghostly, there *is* nothing to see. Barnardo, Marcellus, and Horatio are left begging for the ghost to speak. Variations on the words "Stay! speak, speak! I charge thee, speak!," are repeated twelve times in act 1. If there is nothing to see, then that nothing is charged with speech. What follows, as we have shown, is that nothing of the truth is spoken while speech abounds everywhere, speech precisely of nothing.

THEATER

As we saw, Hamlet grasps the Gorgiastic paradox of theater—that it is a deception in which the deceived is wiser than the nondeceived. At first the paradox appalls him, before appealing to him with the conceit of the play within the play. Theater is "all for nothing," a monstrous fiction and conceit that produces crocodile tears in the eyes of hypocrite actors.

OPHELIA

As the play within the play is about to begin, a particularly manic Hamlet unleashes a volley of bizarreness at Claudius, talking of capons, chameleons, and eating the promise-crammed air. Claudius wearily responds, "I have nothing with this answer, Hamlet. The words are not mine"; to which Hamlet quips, "No, nor mine now." Refusing to sit next to his mother, Hamlet lies at Ophelia's feet, but his words turn obscenely toward her lap and to what lies beneath it:

> HAMLET: Do you think I meant country matters?
> OPHELIA: I think nothing, my lord.
> HAMLET: That's a fair thought to lie between maids' legs.
> OPHELIA: What is, my lord?
> HAMLET: Nothing.
> OPHELIA: You are merry, my lord.

As a venerable tradition of philosophical misogyny insists, extending back to Aristotle's patriarchal biology in *De Generatione Animalium,* the vagina is a thing of nothing, a negative to phallic positivity. It is both the hollow *O* in "Ophelia" and in "For O, for O, the hobby-horse is forgot." The female sexual organs are also identified with matter, which only receive form and life through the pneumatic spark of male semen—country matters is therefore a pleonasm.

But then, as ever in Shakespeare, matters immediately flip around. When Ophelia politely asks what the silent dumbshow at the beginning of *The Mouse-trap* means, Hamlet replies with a slew of lewd puns on the *sh* diagraph:

> HAMLET: Ay, or any show that you'll show him. Be not you ashamed to show, he'll not shame to tell you what it means.
> OPHELIA: You are naught, you are naught: I'll mark the play.

The truth is that Hamlet is naught, both naughty and nothing, a naughty naught, a zero, a whoreson zed, an *O.*

GERTRUDE

The word "nothing" acquires an ever-increasing imperative force and velocity in *Hamlet.* The next series of "nothings" occurs in the extraordinary scene with his mother. After asking why Hamlet speaks to the nothing of the ghost and bends his eye on "vacancy," Gertrude adds:

> GERTRUDE: To whom do you speak this?
> HAMLET: Do you see nothing there?

She replies like a true scholastic philosopher trained in Aristotle:

GERTRUDE: Nothing at all. Yet all that is I see.
HAMLET: Nor did you nothing hear?
GERTRUDE: No, nothing but ourselves.

Gertrude sees nothing and hears nothing and concludes that the ghost is nothing but "the very coinage of your brain" and "ecstasy," which then precipitates Hamlet's explosion of more daggerlike language. She thinks her son is as mad as the sea and wind, but she would. Her passions are not the nothing that is the very coinage of one's brain but the base utility of a woman who satisfies her whims with what merely is, at her will. Hamlet even tries to reduce his mother to this zero point, the time when the heyday in the blood is tame and waits upon the judgment, but she hears none of it.

ROSENCRANTZ AND GUILDENSTERN

If Hamlet is mad, then this doesn't prevent him from elaborating a subtle dialectical critique of the feudal theory of kingship, where the king is identified with the body politic, and the king's *real,* as was said in Elizabethan English, is a realm both real and royal. The limits of the king's body—which is two bodies in one: part human and part divine—are the frontiers of the state, whose ceiling is heaven itself. Deliberately subverting the entreaties of Rosencrantz and Guildenstern (or Rossencraft and Gilderstone, as they are called in the First Quarto, who become Rosincrance and Guyldensterne in the Folio), when they ask where he has hidden the body of Polonius and demand that he come with them to see King Claudius, Hamlet replies,

HAMLET: The body is with the King, but the King is not with the body. The King is a thing—

GUILDENSTERN: A thing, my lord!
HAMLET: Of nothing. Bring me to him. Hide fox,
and all after.

At which point, the hunted Hamlet simply runs away.
As well he might, for this is treason. The king cannot be
nothing. He is the something of somethings: the totality,
the whole, the all, as certain German philosophers
were wont to say. Hamlet is denying the legitimacy of
Claudius's kingship by refusing the identification of the
king with the body of the body politic. The true king is
a ghost (i.e., a nothing), and Claudius is a king of shreds
and patches (i.e., he is nothing). Notice the strange
economy of nothingness here: Gertrude declares to
Hamlet that the ghost of her dead husband is nothing.
Just two scenes later, Hamlet, taking over her words as
always, declares that the new king is nothing.

Indeed, although Hamlet is not physically onstage
at the time, having just left to visit his mother, he
appears to be responding here to Rosencrantz's political theology of majesty,

> The cess of majesty
> Dies not alone; but, like a gulf, doth draw
> What's near it with it. It is a massy wheel,
> Fixed on the summit of the highest mount,
> To whose huge spoke ten thousand lesser things
> Are mortised and adjoined, which when it fall,
> Each small annexment (petty consequence!)
> Attends the boist'rous ruin. Never alone
> Did the King sigh, but with a general groan.

The body of the king is the body politic, and when
the king dies, there is the real, royal risk that the state
will die with him. This is why the king must have two

bodies, one corporeal and the other divine, which means that although the physical substance of kingship is mortal its metaphysical substance is immortal. This is the apparent paradox contained in the words "The king is dead, long live the king." In an image that recurs in *Hamlet,* the king is the *jointure* of the state, and the time is out of joint because the usurper king is that nothing who brought to nothing the true king and stole Hamlet's inheritance.

FORTINBRAS

Hamlet is sent to England to be murdered. Just before he disappears from the stage, there is a short but extraordinary scene on a plain in Denmark, which is slashed to a mere eight lines in the Folio edition.[2] The frame of the scene is war, a futile territorial and religious war, between the Protestant Norwegians led by Fortinbras and the Catholic Poles. Hamlet inquires of a captain in Fortinbras's army as to the substance of the conflict, and he replies, "We go to gain a little patch of ground / That hath in it no profit but the name." Yet the patch of ground is garrisoned with what Hamlet imagines—although he is never given this information—as "Two thousand souls and twenty thousand ducats." Oddly, thirty-five lines farther on, Hamlet substitutes souls for ducats and exaggeratingly speaks of "The imminent death of twenty thousand men."

Hamlet then asks to be left alone for a moment and soliloquizes for the last time. The pattern of the soliloquy closely resembles that of the meditation on theater from act 2, which here becomes a theater of war. He ruminates on the essential nihilism of war, where twenty thousand men go to their deaths for nothing, for "a fantasy and trick of fame." But then he finds in the spectacle yet more motivation for his promised act of revenge:

> How do all occasions inform against me
> And spur my dull revenge.

He continues:

> Witness this army of such mass and charge
> Led by a delicate and tender prince,
> Whose spirit with divine ambition puffed
> Makes mouths at the invisible event.

Is it not odd that Hamlet denigrates Fortinbras as a "delicate and tender" puff and then with his dying words advocates for his succession as king of Denmark? Be that as it may, Hamlet's familiar line of reasoning here is the following: seeing twenty thousand men led by a dainty, puffed-up prince fight over nothing but a "quarrel in a straw," Hamlet asks himself "How stand I then?" If twenty thousand men are prepared to fight over nothing, then how can one man who has genuine cause for action, such as himself, *do* nothing? Therefore, he concludes, he must do something.

He ends the soliloquy with the words "My thoughts be bloody, or be nothing worth!" And with that, he disappears until act 5. Now, there is no doubt that Hamlet's thoughts are bloody. He fantasizes repeatedly about an act of ultraviolent vengeance that must be performed at exactly the right time. But that time never comes. Hamlet never lives in his own time. The problem does not lie with Hamlet's thoughts but with his acts.

Of course, Hamlet being Hamlet knows this with

the lucidity of a philosophical anthropologist. Earlier in the soliloquy, anticipating the culminating question of Kant's critical system, he asks, "What is a man?" The answer, of course, is a rational animal. The human being is divided between the beastly need to feed and God-given reason and the capacity for "large discourse." So, Hamlet ratiocinates, which part of us causes inhibition at the level of action? He ponders,

> Now, whether it be
> Bestial oblivion, or some craven scruple
> Of thinking too precisely on th' event—
> A thought, which quartered, hath but one part
> wisdom
> And ever three parts coward—I do not know
> Why yet I live to say "This thing's to do,"
> Sith I have cause, and will, and strength, and means
> To do't. Examples gross as earth exhort me.

There are perhaps no more poignant words in *Hamlet* than these: he simply does not know whether it is animalistic cowardice or the fault that flows from an excess of thought that prevents him from the act of revenge. He has cause, will, strength, and means, and he can mumble to himself, like a character in a Nike commercial, "Just do it." But nothing happens. It's like the moment at the end of both acts of *Waiting for Godot* when first Vladimir and then Estragon say, "Yes, let's go." Beckett's stage direction reads *[They do not move]*.

LAERTES

Laertes is Hamlet's rival, the double he both deeply admires and who functions as a kind of mirror in which Hamlet begins to glimpse the filaments of his desire. During the final, fatal rapier match, the "water-fly" courtier Osric declares, "Nothing neither way." These words describe with precision their intense loving hatred, their frenmity. There is "nothing neither way" to choose between them.

What Hamlet and Laertes have in common, which brings them together and tears them apart, is a love of Ophelia, debased in life only to be elevated in death. Immediately after Hamlet departs for England, there follows a curious scene that begins with Gertrude refusing to speak with Ophelia, "I will not speak with her." However, within fifteen lines, after hearing the arguments of an unnamed gentleman, Gertrude changes her mind and declares, "Let her come in." What sways her is the potent political threat that Ophelia poses. "Her speech is nothing," the gentleman insists, and "nothing sure," but "it doth move / The hearers to collection." Ophelia, raving in psychotic grief, in "winks, and nods, and gestures," suggests that Gertrude and Claudius are responsible for her father's murder. In the nothing of Ophelia's speech something is heard, standing in such strange contrast to the general deafness of Elsinore castle.

Horatio then advises Gertrude to see Ophelia because she may "strew dangerous conjectures in ill-breeding minds." This might give one pause: What exactly is Horatio doing in this scene at all? Is he truly Hamlet's bosom buddy, or has he somehow become Gertrude's close counselor? It is not at all clear. Indeed, in the Folio edition, the part of the gentleman is elided, and the scene becomes an intimate tête-à-tête between Horatio and the queen.

But the real nature of Ophelia's threat is revealed as

she is exiting this scene. After a flow of seeming non-sense and mad song, she simply adds, "My brother shall know of it." However, it appears that Laertes is already fully aware of the situation and about to storm the king's palace in the next scene. The winks, nods, and gestures of Ophelia have already insinuated themselves into the ear of Laertes, as Claudius readily admits:

> Wherein necessity, of matter beggared,
> Will nothing stick our person to arraign
> In ear and ear.

When Laertes and Ophelia meet onstage for the first time since their father's death, she comes a-singing, armed with flowers. She speaks, "It is the false steward that stole his master's daughter." Laertes responds, as if to Claudius's words above, "This nothing's more than matter."

The most insurrectionary political threats in *Hamlet* are nothings that are more than matter and that circulate from ear to ear, ghostlike, outside the control of the king and his warlike, massy-wheeled state. The nothing of Ophelia echoes Hamlet's insistence on the king as a thing of nothing. In short, there is a palpable political threat in *Hamlet* that operates through a double negation: to bring to nothing that which is—the matter of the usurper king's state—and to see that which is from the standpoint of a nothing that exceeds it: the ghostly, the spectral, which is also the order of truth and justice, the truth of what happened to Hamlet Senior and the justice of the act of retributive revenge. In order to rebut this threat, Claudius engages in a wonderful example of that quintessential political act—lying—in order to turn Laertes's rage away from him and toward the final showdown with Hamlet. Claudius argues that if Laertes is to truly show himself Polonius's son, then he must kill Hamlet—prove your love with murder!

HORATIO

In a heartfelt declaration of love, Hamlet says to Horatio:

> For thou hast been
> As one, in suff'ring all, that suffers nothing . . .

It is certainly true that Horatio has to suffer Hamlet's tangled knot of nothings throughout the play. And this is nowhere truer than in the cluster of negations that appear in the "We defy augury" speech we looked at above: "If it be now, 'tis not to come. If it be not to come, it will be now. If it be not now, yet it will come," and so on.

How might one understand the "not" here, the "nothing"? Hamlet goes on, "Since man, of aught he leaves, knows aught, what is't to leave betimes?" No man knows aught of aught he leaves. Therefore, to follow Hamlet's reasoning, we know naught. We know nothing. When Hamlet concludes, "Let be," does this mean let naught be? Let nothing be? Recall that the ghost—who is nothing—accurately reports: "Let me be."

The readiness that is all is a readiness for the "not" that will come and become now. We must hold ourselves ready for it and, to use Edgar's word from the end of *King Lear,* endure. We must hold ourselves ready for nothing. This is what we earlier called a disposition of skeptical openness. We must not claim to know aught of what we truly know naught.

Does this mean that Hamlet is a nihilist? After his

cunning escape from the fatal clutches of Rosencrantz and Guildenstern, many readers insist that Hamlet has changed. They claim that he has thrown off his madness; his "antic disposition" disappears; he appears more mature and resolute. In Harold Bloom's words,

> What seems clear is that the urgency of the earlier Hamlet has gone. Instead, a mysterious and beautiful disinterestedness dominates this truer Hamlet, who compels a universal love.[3]

Is it really *clear* that Hamlet has changed? Do the ever-shifting melancholia and mania of the earlier Hamlet yield to a truer and more beautiful disinterestedness? Is Hamlet someone who, at the end of the tragedy, compels universal love? To understate matters somewhat, we are not convinced. Is Hamlet really so different when he returns from his passage to England? Is he really more resolute and less crazy? And if he is so utterly changed, then why does he immediately leap into Ophelia's grave and wrestle wildly with Laertes? If he is suddenly so disinterested, then why does the "bravery" of Laertes's grief put Hamlet into such a "tow'ring passion," as he later confesses to Horatio? Does such behavior not betray a certain ugly interest rather than beautiful disinterest? Why does Hamlet rave at Laertes—"Woo't weep? Woo't fight? Woo't fast? Woo't tear thyself? Woo't drink up eisel? eat a crocodile?"—before being wrongly declared mad by Gertrude in exactly the same, stupid, misguided way as she said earlier when her son saw the ghost? Does Hamlet compel universal love? Or are we not reluctantly obliged to conclude that Hamlet is really not such a nice guy? That all his beautiful contemplation is for nothing?

For Bloom, any "apparent nihilism" on the part of Hamlet gives way to "achieved serenity" and "authentic disinterestedness."[4] In fact he goes so far as to say that Hamlet is a resurrected Christ figure during act 5, at the same time that he represents an Old Testament Adamic truth, "There is a God within him and he speaks: 'and yet, to me, what is this quintessence of dust?' Hamlet's is the most refined of all Adamic dusts, but remains the Old Adam and not the New: essentially dust."[5] This sounds delightful, if not completely contradictory, but all in all it is the assurance of the claim to authenticity, old or new—and thereby to a certain moral standard for what might count as the humanity that Shakespeare allegedly invents—that we doubt and that fails to see the sheer weirdness of the play. We here concur with Melville's hero, Pierre:

> Pierre had always been an admiring reader of *Hamlet;* but neither his age nor his mental experience thus far, had qualified him either to catch initiating glimpses into *the hopeless gloom of its interior meaning,* or to draw from the general story those superficial and purely incidental lessons, where the pains-taking moralist so complacently expatiates.[6]

Pierre then tears his copy of *Hamlet* into "a hundred shreds" and drops them at his feet.[7]

Part I

By Indirections Find Directions Out—
Carl Schmitt's Hamletization

WHY IS HAMLET unable to speak the truth about what he has learned from the lips of the ghost? Why is Hamlet unable to utter to anyone onstage what he has heard, not even to ever-loyal Horatio? Why the desperate need for secrecy? In 1955, Carl Schmitt, the infamous German jurist, gave a series of lectures, entitled *Hamlet or Hecuba,* that circle obsessively around these questions.

To understate matters somewhat alarmingly, Schmitt is a controversial figure. Although this is not the place, much could and should be said about his involvement with the National Socialist regime and his apologia for dictatorship and political authoritarianism. But let's initially confine ourselves to one line of questioning. Schmitt is best known as the great theorist of the decision, where the concept of the political consists in the ability to decide between friend and enemy. Schmitt's famous definition of sovereignty is, in a literal translation, "Sovereign is, who can decide on the state of exception" (*Souverän ist, wer über den Ausnahmezustand entscheidet*). The sovereign is the person who is exhibited by the decision on the state of exception. The question "who?" is answered by the decision itself. That is, the decision on the state of exception, the moment of the suspension of the operation of law, brings the subject "who?" into being. To put it into a slogan, *the subject is the consequence of a decision.* Thus, the subject of political sovereignty—a prince of Denmark, for example, and would-be king—is defined, indeed constituted, by the potent capacity for decision. The sovereign has to be politically and—insofar as the body politic is identified with the body of the king—corporeally virile.

The question then becomes blindingly obvious: if the decision is so decisive to the very definition of politics and sovereignty, then what on earth is Carl Schmitt—Herr Professor Dr. Decision Himself—doing focusing on the most indecisive character in world literature: Hamlet? As Hamlet already made crystal clear above, he cannot act on the basis of the instructions of the ghost and avenge his father's murder. Now, if sovereignty is the capacity for a decision, then is indecision a questioning of sovereignty? If the political is defined by the sovereign decision, then does the indecision of the sovereign—and Hamlet is rightful heir to the rotten state of Denmark—imply a critique of this concept of the political? If the sovereign is defined by the potency of decision, then is Hamlet's evident impotence somehow politically important? Does this indecision mark a crisis in the concept of sovereignty? Or can we perhaps imagine an uncoupling of sovereignty from potency and a shift in the classical conception of the political subject? Is it too much of a stretch to say that Schmitt's meditation on Hamlet might be read as a kind of critique of his earlier decisionistic conceptions of politics and sovereignty? Might Schmitt's *Hamlet or Hecuba* be read, then, as an oblique self-critique?

Be that as it may—and the latter questions are admittedly speculative—what is certain is that Hamlet cannot decide: for whatever reason, he's lost his mojo of sovereign potency. As we said above, Hamlet is an anti-Oedipus. Where Oedipus begins knowing nothing and acts constantly till he is led toward the knowledge that destroys him, Hamlet knows everything from the get-go. What is revealed is that this knowledge does not lead to action but to its opposite. On this account, the character of the tragic hero shifts decisively from antiquity to modernity: the modern hero cannot decide. This is the process that Schmitt Germanizes with what Polonius would call a "vile phrase": Hamletization (*Hamletisierung*). It might turn out that this term best describes the condition into which the political has fallen in the modern world: we have all become indecisive Hamlets living in states that we know to be rotten. Perhaps Schmitt's decisionistic concept of the political has become Hamletized.

But why is Hamlet Hamletized? Why does he remain tight lipped about what he knows? While vigorously disavowing the validity of any psychoanalytic interpretations of *Hamlet*—indeed "the lady doth protest too much, methinks"—Schmitt nonetheless insists that what we are faced with in the play is, to use a Freudian term, "a taboo."[1] For Schmitt, there are two riddles in the play: first, Hamlet's indecisiveness and inability to avenge his father, and, second, the lack of clarity as to the guilt or innocence of Gertrude.

Both riddles are solved by linking the taboo not to what Schmitt would see as some vague psychoanalytic cause but to a real historical situation. Schmitt's basic claim is that Hamlet is a mask for King James I of England. James's mother was Mary, Queen of Scots, whose husband, Henry Stuart, Lord Darnley, was murdered fewer than eight months after James's birth in June 1566. Mary remarried three months after her husband's murder, with James Hepburn, fourth Earl of Bothwell, who was widely suspected of being the murderer of Henry Stuart.

In February 1601, the Earl of Essex, together with the Earl of Southampton, led an abortive rebellion against the aging and increasingly despotic Queen Elizabeth, Essex's former mentor and probable lover. The rebellion failed, Essex was beheaded, and Southampton's death sentence was commuted to life imprisonment. Now, both Essex and Southampton were active patrons of Shakespeare's acting troupe, the Lord Chamberlain's Men. After the event of the rebellion, very possibly alluded to as "the late innovation" in *Hamlet,* the theaters were closed, ostensibly because of the plague. This explains why "the tragedians of the city" are wandering the country in search of employment. During this period, there was also a sudden mode for children's acting companies, such as the Children of the Chapel, referred to explicitly in *Hamlet* as "Little eyases, that cry out on the top of question, and are most tyrannically clapped for't."

Any precise dating of *Hamlet* is necessarily speculative, and we would rather avoid the distracting and unending quest for an authentic and original *Ur-Hamlet.* We know that on July 26, 1602, Shakespeare's *Hamlet* was entered in the Stationer's Register in London, and the play must have been performed prior to that date. The First, or so-called bad, Quarto, which has many odd virtues, not the least of which is a kind of rough-and-ready theatricality that is close to tragic farce, was published in 1603, the year of James's accession to the throne. The Second Quarto, sometimes jokingly called *Hamlet* in its eternity rather than entirety, was published in 1604–5 and is 79 percent longer than the First. After James became monarch of both England and Scotland, the Lord Chamberlain's Men became the King's Men, and Shakespeare was appointed royal valet. Schmitt's claim, then, is that *Hamlet* harbors a taboo, and this provides the reason that the play takes on its peculiarly oblique form. Schmitt writes that, out of consideration for King James, "it was impossible to insinuate the *guilt* of the mother in the murder of the father."[2]

Schmitt provides an admittedly singular and, indeed, odd taboo-based explanation of Hamlet's Hamletization, which it is impossible either to refute or confirm. A little like Hamlet himself, Schmitt cannot bear the sheer fictional Gorgiastic deceptiveness of theater, its nothing. The power of an artwork cannot therefore be explained in exclusively aesthetic terms but must be located in a specific historical reality. His interpretation has the virtue of explaining the great success of *Hamlet* on the London stage: everyone knew that it was the true backstory of the new king, but no one could say this openly. *Hamlet* is a kind of *pièce à clé*.

This Globe of Spies

BUT DO WE need such a determinate, external historical explanation of *Hamlet* in order to throw light on the
phenomenon of Hamletization? After all, there might
be other reasons for Hamlet's silence that are internal to
the play itself. In order to broach this line of thought,
let's go back to the beginning of *Hamlet*. In the final
scene of act 1, after Hamlet's encounter with the ghost,
he swears that he shall avenge his father's murder,

> Thy commandment all alone shall live
> Within the book and volume of my brain

Hamlet then hears the voices of Horatio and Marcellus
seeking him out. Horatio shouts "Hillo, ho, ho, my
lord!" to which Hamlet responds ecstatically, "Hillo,
ho, ho, boy! Come, bird, come." When Horatio asks
for news of what's happened, Hamlet cries out sponta-
neously and manically, "O, wonderful!" But then when
Horatio asks Hamlet to tell the news, Hamlet's response
becomes instantly guarded, "No, you will reveal it."
There then follows some sixty rather agonizing lines
of back and forth between Hamlet, Horatio, and the
others, where the ghost intervenes no fewer than four
times, demanding that they "Swear by his sword."

But what are they swearing to keep secret? To be
sure, it is *not* the secret that Hamlet has heard about

his father's murder, because he does not tell it to them. All that they swear to keep secret is presumably that a ghost appeared who bears an extraordinary resemblance to the dead king. True enough, in act 3 Hamlet alludes to "the circumstance / Which I have told thee, of my father's death." But we are not witnesses to what Horatio is told. We don't know what he knows. As events move toward their denouement in act 5, Hamlet once again assumes that Horatio knows, although he does not utter the secret onstage.

Why the need for secrecy? A possible answer is provided by the very scene that follows Hamlet's encounter with the ghost, in the seemingly incidental opening lines of act 2. Polonius is in conversation with one Reynaldo (the cunning Reynard, or fox, who becomes Reynoldo in the Folio edition and Montano in the First Quarto, where Polonius is mysteriously transformed into Corambis, which is apparently the name for a genus of spider), whom he is hiring to spy on his son, Laertes, who has just returned to Paris. Mightn't it strike us as odd that the very same Polonius, who had given his son such sage fatherly advice in act 1 as "Neither a borrower nor a lender be" and "To thine own self be true" should now be sending a spy to follow him? Furthermore, the ruse here is wickedly artful: Polonius asks Reynaldo to insinuate himself with certain Danish friends of Laertes in Paris, "Danskers" (which is accurate: "Danish" is *Dansk* in Danish), and to "put on him / What forgeries you please." To be clear, Reynaldo is meant to tell lies about Laertes, such as "drinking, fencing, swearing, quarelling, / Drabbing," that is, whoring. Polonius's reasoning is quite bizarre and couched in fishing and hunting metaphors:

Your bait of falsehood takes this carp of truth,
And thus do we of wisdom and of reach
With windlasses and with assays of bias,
By indirections find directions out.

Fishing here is really *phishing,* the elaborate construction of a hoax to take in the gullible, in this case
Laertes's Parisian Dansker chums. Reynaldo is paid to
tell lies in order to see if they reveal anything sordid but
true in Laertes's behavior. Why is the lie always the only
path to the truth? And further, it is not even enough
just to spy—as if we slide between the meanings of the
word "insinuate."

Hamlet's world is a globe defined by the omnipresence of espionage. *Hamlet* is arguably the drama
of surveillance in a police state, rather like the Elizabethan police state of England in the late sixteenth
century or the multitude of surveillance cameras that
track citizens as they cross London in the current second late-Elizabethan age. Indeed, during the time of
the Cold War, in countries like Poland and Czechoslo-
vakia, *Hamlet* was not seen as some existential drama
of indecision in a world of bourgeois anomie but as
an allegory of life in a totalitarian regime. The First
Quarto version of *Hamlet* was famously performed
as something between tragedy and absurdist farce in
1978 at the Theatre on the Balustrade in Prague, where
Václav Havel started as a stagehand. In this interpretation, Polonius has the key role as spymaster general.

Consider the proliferation of spies in *Hamlet:* Rosencrantz and Guildenstern are sent to spy on Hamlet;
Ophelia agrees to be the bait as Claudius and Polonius spy on the prince; Polonius spies a second time
and is undone with a rapier; someone is clearly spying

on Ophelia, otherwise an account of her last moments before she slipped into "muddy death" could not have been given. And is there not the slightest doubt as to the integrity of Horatio—oh so loyal and beloved Horatio—who suddenly turns up out of the blue from Wittenberg to attend Hamlet Senior's funeral and has apparently been hanging around Elsinore for two months somehow unnoticed by Hamlet (how big *is* Elsinore?). As well as being on friendly terms with the sentinels, Marcellus and Barnardo, Horatio also seems to recognize Hamlet Senior in the armor he wore in a battle that was fought some thirty years earlier (presumably before he was born).

Isn't this all very odd? Might not Horatio be Fortinbras's spy? Think about it: the play finishes with a cordial exchange between Horatio and Fortinbras where the latter declares, "Bear Hamlet like a soldier to the stage." But in this interpretation, such magnanimity is not surprising because Hamlet has served as the perfect, albeit unknowing, conduit by which Fortinbras could accede to the throne of Denmark. The pretender Hamlet murders Claudius but has the decency to kill himself in the process and with his "dying voice" says "th'election lights / On Fortinbras." Take it a step further: let's imagine that Horatio and his paid accomplices, Marcellus and Barnardo, agree to concoct the story of the ghost in order to dupe an already intensely fragile, grief-stricken, and almost-suicidal young aristocrat. Hamlet unwittingly adds the patina of psychotic delusion to their deception, and this is more than enough to motivate the young prince to kill his uncle and clear the path for Fortinbras. Horatio knows everything from the get-go because Hamlet is his puppet and the ghost is his ruse.

This last hypothesis is admittedly slightly far-fetched, although arguably no more so than Schmitt's taboo interpretation. But the point is that everyone is being watched in *Hamlet,* and everyone lives in fear because they *know* they are being watched. And, of course, to add one obvious extra layer of espionage, we watch this world of spies while being spies ourselves, sitting there in what Hamlet calls "this distracted globe," meaning both the Globe Theatre and the *theatrum mundi,* which is the macrocosm of theater's microcosm. The globe is a panopticon.

Elsinore is a world of spies, a world of utter political mistrust in a corrupt and murderous regime defined by the constant threat of war, a "warlike state," as Claudius says in his opening speech, whose "imperial jointress" is Gertrude (so if the time is out of joint, as Hamlet says, then something is awry with the state's *maternal* function). The frame of *Hamlet* is war, and the usurper Claudius has two enemies: the external enemy of Fortinbras and the internal enemy whose identity wheels around in the play, from Hamlet to Laertes, in accordance with Claudius's paranoid—but astutely accurate—political sensibility.

He Is Not a Nice Guy—
Hamlet as Prince and Political Threat

THE WORRY ABOUT Hamlet is not really his madness, feigned or otherwise. Claudius never believes for a moment Polonius's lay analytic etiology of Hamlet's distracted aspect—namely, his purported love for Ophelia. "Love? His affections do not that way tend," Claudius says. Hamlet constitutes a *political* threat, and his madness is simply a cover for "some danger." This is why Claudius invokes the conceit of the Danegeld, the tribute of money historically paid by England to Denmark to stop the latter plundering the former. Before he has even heard out Polonius's psychoanalytic interpretation of Hamlet's disturbance of the erotic function, Claudius declares that he has already written letters determining that Hamlet "shall with speed to England" in order to be executed. The worry about Hamlet is that he has popular support, the people like him: "He's loved of the distracted multitude."

So too with the threat from that other internal enemy, Laertes—Hamlet's rival and, in many respects, uncanny double (we will come back to that). After he hears of Polonius's murder, Laertes returns in secret from France and suspects that Claudius is culpable of the crime. Again, Claudius's fear is political:

The people muddied,
Thick and unwholesome in their thoughts and
whispers,
For good Polonius' death.

Claudius's fears are immediately confirmed. "The rabble call him lord," the gentleman reports. "They cry, 'Choose we! Laertes shall be king!'" In the only really insurrectionary moment in the play, Laertes bursts violently into the castle determined to murder the supposed murderer of his father. What is so striking in this violent confrontation—"O thou vile king"—is the ice-cold clarity of Claudius, who slowly turns Laertes's anger around onto Hamlet and inveigles him into the plot of the poisoned foils that will cost them both their lives.

For Hamlet, "Denmark's a prison." Indeed, as he goes on to add, the whole distracted globe is a "goodly" or capacious prison. Spies are everywhere; political intrigue and violence surround Hamlet and threaten to engulf him. The omnipresence of spies engenders an attitude of utter mistrust that consumes Hamlet's soul, rendering him incapable of love. *Hamlet* is a political tragedy in the most intense sense. If there is one mood that governs all others in the play, then it is *fear*. Once the layers of growing paranoia in the play are peeled back, this is where Laertes's initial advice in act 1 to Ophelia before he departs for Paris becomes prescient. Although Laertes acknowledges that Hamlet might indeed love Ophelia now, he counsels her, "But you must fear." This is because Hamlet is the future sovereign and "his will is not his own." On Hamlet's will "depends the safety and health of this whole state." The state of Denmark is that body whereof Hamlet is "the head." And the head can only choose what is in the interest of the general health of the body politic. If Ophelia loses her honor to Hamlet or opens the "chaste treasure" of her virginity, then she will have lost her only hope of an advantageous marriage and social advancement. Hamlet might and indeed possibly must choose another to marry in order to forge a political alliance that best serves the Danish state. If she reciprocates his love, she risks everything. Laertes adds, "Fear it, Ophelia, fear it, my dear sister"—the closer to Caesar, the greater the fear.

Laertes is correct. Hamlet is not some obsessionally indecisive petit bourgeois everyman. He is not, in an interpretation that Goethe's *Wilhelm Meister* made famous, "A fine, pure, noble and highly moral person" who is burdened with a task that is impossible for him. Hamlet is not a *nice guy*. He is not someone with whom we should simplemindedly identify because his dad's been killed and his mum's a woman of opportunistic and easy virtue.

An attentive reading of the play shows the *princely* quality of Hamlet. He is heir to the throne and should have ascended to it after his namesake father's death. Hamlet is a sovereign in waiting who does not want to wait, but nonetheless hesitates in his revenge. He is a real political threat to Claudius and someone who knows that he is threatened at each and every moment with the same fate as his father: assassination. As prince and pretender, Hamlet is a potentially malevolent force who should be feared, which—reflexively—is why he lives in fear. Ophelia is from a different social rank, the daughter of a bureaucrat, and, as Polonius acknowledges, Hamlet "is a prince, out of thy star." Incidentally, perhaps this gives the lie to Polonius's stubbornly held hypothesis about Hamlet's love for Ophelia. If the hypothesis can be proven, then they might be married, in which case Polonius would ascend from the rank of courtier to that of father of the queen.

There are wheels within wheels in this play, and they all spin around the blinding sun of political power. Boethius's image of the Wheel of Fortune here becomes what Rosencrantz calls the "massy wheel" of majesty whose governing political virtue is *fortuna,* or "luck." The sheer contingency of political life requires masses of luck. We might recall the apocryphal story that Boethius's *Consolation of Philosophy* was translated by Queen Elizabeth from the Latin in a period of twenty-four hours. Lucky girl.

Is Hamlet *a Tragedy or a* Trauerspiel?

CARL SCHMITT'S interpretation of *Hamlet* betrays a certain plodding flat-footedness. But he has the great virtue of not pretending to be what he isn't. In the final part of *Hamlet or Hecuba,* which is by far the most interesting part of the book, he considers the following question: Should historical arguments ever be included in the consideration of a work of art? Schmitt criticizes any idea of the artwork as hermetically sealed from history but also acknowledges, "I do not expect anyone to think of James I when Hamlet is on stage."[3]

Schmitt's views on the relation between art and history are informed by and form a complex crisscrossing pattern with a second outsider interpreter of *Hamlet:* Walter Benjamin. *The Origin of German Tragic Drama* (1928)—which famously failed in its intention of qualifying Benjamin for a professorship in Germany—is a study of *Trauerspiel* (mourning play), which was a form of drama that flourished in the Germanophone world in the period of the Counter-Reformation in the late sixteenth and early seventeenth centuries, the period during which Shakespeare was writing, acting, and directing. Benjamin's *Trauerspiel* book, especially its "Epistemo-Critical Prologue," boasts a ferocious complexity of utterance and presentation. In many ways, the baroque, allegorical, densely allusive, cumulative style of the book's form is an image of the content of

Trauerspiel that Benjamin wants to defend and that will inform his style in his last, posthumously published, work, *The Arcades Project.*

Benjamin relentlessly undermines any symbolic conception of art—common in romantic aesthetics, where the particular serves as a vehicle for the purportedly universal—with a notion of allegory, where we seek the particular *in* the universal. If the symbolic is the possibility of a redemptive artwork, the mystical *scintilla dei* when the clouds part and we suddenly see the face of God or the vibrant totality of nature or indeed both, as in Wordsworth's ascent of Snowdon in *The Prelude,* then the allegorical is the petrified and primordial landscape of a ruined history that finds expression in a death's head: Yorick's skull. The literature of the baroque is a ceaseless piling up of fragments, like the stage full of corpses at the end of *Hamlet.* If the symbolic artist surveys the wonder of the universe prior to merging with it, then the baroque allegorist spends years in musty libraries, melancholically mulling over "words, words, words." As its name suggests, the overwhelming mood of *Trauerspiel* is mourning, and at its center stands the figure of the pensive and melancholic prince.

The question obviously arises as to whether or not *Hamlet* is a *Trauerspiel.* Neither Schmitt nor Benjamin think so but for very different and indeed contradictory reasons. Benjamin makes a rather-broad and ad hoc distinction between *Trauerspiel* and tragedy. His initial organizing claim is that history is the content of *Trauerspiel* whereas myth is the content of tragedy. Namely, *Trauerspiel* is not concerned with the tragic conflict with the gods and the power of fate, some prehistoric conflict out of which the polis emerges as in the *Oresteia,* at least in a certain interpretation. Rather, *Trauerspiel* is the drama of the sovereign as the physical incarnation of history. Benjamin writes that the sovereign, for example, the prince, "holds the course of history in his hand like a sceptre."[4] At this point, an odd thing happens in Benjamin's book: he alludes directly to Schmitt's 1922 book, *Political Theology.* We will see this allusion spin back to Schmitt before he hurls it, boomeranglike, to knock over Benjamin's argument. The claim is that *Trauerspiel* is coextensive with the emergence of the modern concept of sovereignty understood by Schmitt as the capacity to decide on the state of exception. Yet, the sovereign hero of *Trauerspiel,* like Hamlet, is radically indecisive: he cannot decide; he cannot act in the appropriately sovereign manner that would arrest the empty flow of historical time with the iron fist of dictatorship.

So, the question comes back: Why is *Hamlet,* the great drama of sovereign indecision, not a *Trauerspiel*? Indeed, the play would seem to correspond to two other elements in addition to history by which Benjamin seeks to distinguish tragedy from *Trauerspiel:*

1. If murder in ancient tragedy is *sacrifice,* then in modern tragedy—and Hegel also makes this claim—it is simple criminality. There is nothing sacrificial in the murder of Hamlet Senior; it is a crime committed in order to achieve the goal of political power.

2. For Benjamin, *silence* is central to the heroes of ancient tragedy and "constitutes the sublime element in tragedy." By contrast, the hero of *Trauerspiel* is possessed of an endless mad chatter. The incapacity for action on the part of the hero seems to be linked

to the propensity for talk, for twitter, for the empty birdsong of signifiers. We cannot act because our mouths are always full of words, words, words.

Myth, sacrifice, and *silence*—although it is not our main purpose here, it would be relatively easy to dismantle each of Benjamin's criteria for distinguishing ancient tragedy from modern *Trauerspiel* by showing its presence in Attic tragedy. For example, the oldest extant piece of theater that we possess, Aeschylus's *The Persians,* from 472 BCE (which also features a ghost, that of Darius the Great—the spectacle of theater begins with a specter) does not deal with myth but with historical fact, indeed the very recent historical fact of the aftermath of the Battle of Salamis that happened eight years prior to the first performance of the play at the City Dionysia in Athens.

Other examples of the presence of history in ancient tragedy and the complex *anachronism* of the time of history and the time of myth could be given. Ancient tragedy is self-consciously anachronistic, producing a kind of disjunction in the order of time. Characters from the mythic past are presented dealing with contemporary crises of legitimacy—for example, between the claims of family and city. Or again, in the *Oresteia* we see goddesses like Athena from the distant Mycenaean past employing the very latest rhetorical techniques of sophistic, legal argumentation. This is a little like Milton being summoned to invoke the intricacies of the current U.S. tax code.

Attic tragedy is about neither just the past nor the present, the time of myth and the time of law, but their inextricable and fatal entanglement, which leads to disaster. *Hamlet* too proceeds from an anachronism or disjunction between the distant time of the myth of Amhlaide and Amleth in Snorri Sturluson and Saxo Grammaticus to the paranoid reality of political life in late Elizabethan and early Jacobean England.

On the question of sacrifice, it is more than arguable that what we might call the *meta-theater* of Euripides, in play after play, is the exposure of the criminality at the heart of what was meant to pass as sacrifice. Iphigenia was not an offering to the gods; she was a pawn in a game of political sovereignty, and her brutal murder, described even by Aeschylus as like that of a young foal gagged and hoisted high over the altar, was a crime. But after reading Euripides's *Orestes* or *Elektra,* we can be in no doubt that the occupants of the House of Atreus are no less brigands than those in Elsinore.

Finally, although—for obvious reasons—we have no record of the silences in ancient tragedy, and it must be acknowledged that Aristophanes praises Aeschylus in *The Frogs* for his mastery of silence, ancient tragedy is not mired in some prerational, ritualized, and silent stupor as certain readers tend to imagine based on an enthused reading of Nietzsche's *The Birth of Tragedy.* Tragedy is the incessant flow of language and, more particularly, the bivalent rationality of argument and counterargument in the *agon,* or "conflict." Ancient tragedy is awash with words and the back and forth of rational argumentation that keeps abutting impotently against the fact of violence. For example, in Euripides's *Trojan Women,* Cassandra produces textbook examples of sophistic reasoning, perhaps directly influenced by Gorgias, before being given to Agamemnon as booty, taken to Mycenae, and slaughtered—of course, being Cassandra and endowed with the gift of prophecy, she knows all of this from the get-go.

The Mute Rock of Reality

SCHMITT'S ARGUMENT as to why *Hamlet* is tragedy and not *Trauerspiel* is singular and powerful. First, he wants to insist that there is and should be a distinction between tragedy and *Trauerspiel*. Schmitt sees the latter, with Benjamin, as a melancholic form of drama or, more properly, melodrama—that is, a form of play (*Spiel*)—that does not rise to the level of tragedy. For Schmitt, interestingly, the play within the play, *The Mouse-trap*, is a *Trauerspiel*. Its significance derives from the fact that it is a *Trauerspiel* wrapped within a genuine tragedy. *Trauerspiel* becomes tragic when, to cite the subtitle to Schmitt's book, there is an intrusion of time into the play. These intrusions—the taboo surrounding the guilt of the queen and the indecision or Hamletization of the avenging hero—are "shadows, two dark areas."[5] Using what might be seen as a self-consciously ironic Marxist metaphor, Schmitt writes that "genuine tragedy has a special and extraordinary quality, a kind of *surplus value* [emphasis ours] that no play, however, perfect, can attain." He goes on:

> This surplus value lies in the objective reality of the tragic action itself, in the enigmatic concatenation and entanglement of indisputably real people in the unpredictable course of indisputably real events.[6]

Thus, what makes tragic action genuine is a surplus value that arises out of the "mute rock" of historical reality. This reality has a reflexive function that Schmitt describes in a maritime metaphor (the significance of which will soon become clear): reality is the rock "upon which the play founders, sending the foam of genuine tragedy rising to the surface." Thus, the rock of historical reality is the condition of possibility for tragedy, yet that condition cannot be revealed in the play; it has to remain an invisible and unspeakable substratum beneath the sea surface of the drama. True play draws from that which is not in play. Schmitt seems to be working with an implicit distinction between imagination and fancy. If the melodrama of *Trauerspiel* is fancy, or fantasy unanchored in reality, then tragedy is a work of the imagination that draws from, and may even break in upon, a reality that is mute within it.

What is being described here is a limit to invention that is invention's condition of possibility. This limit is the real, understood historically not psychoanalytically—although the structuring function of the real as a material, thingly painful limit resounds across both registers. This raises the question of the psychoanalytic dimension of Schmitt's reading of *Hamlet,* with its emphasis on taboo as the repressed latent content of the drama. The repressed in Schmitt can have the character of a time that is other to the fictive temporal consciousness of the play or, characterized more through content, as Hamlet's incestuous desire that emerges as a preoccupation with Gertrude's guilt. If Schmitt's *Hamlet or Hecuba* can be read as an attempted self-critique of his conceptions of sovereignty and the political, then *Hamlet or Hecuba* might be read as a kind of self-analysis that by indecision finds decisions out.

The tragic writer, or indeed any writer, does not invent the mute rock of reality at the core of true tragedy. An invented fate is no fate at all. Schmitt continues:

> The core of tragic action, the source of tragic authenticity, is something so irrevocable that no mortal can invent it, no genius can produce it out of thin air.[7]

Not even the "incomparable greatness"[8] of Shakespeare can make up a true tragedy out of his own fanciful musings. It finds its source in a reality or, perhaps better and more existentially stated, a *facticity* that faces us with an incontrovertible and implacable force. The hubris of melodrama, no less the hubris of man himself, is to believe that it fashions this facticity, which is, according to Schmitt, why it rings so false. Melodrama is a fortification against the real act. Melodrama's surplus of affect and action disarms the threatening external intrusion of reality into the play itself. Ask a psychoanalyst if this is not something confronted every day on the couch—the distraction of one's own melodramatics.

In ancient Greek tragedy, this is the very facticity of myth, which is neither fable nor play but *fate*. In Shakespeare, on the cusp of what we too simple-mindedly think of as modernity, that facticity is historical reality and, in the case of *Hamlet,* according to Schmitt, the story of James I of England. If ancient tragedy is the transfiguration of mythic fate, in its Homeric or other version, into the novel spectacle of civic, political theater, then modern tragedy is the transfiguration of historical and political reality into the *fatum* of myth. If Sophocles manages to fuse myth with the emerging historical reality of the Athenian polis, then Shakespeare elevates the historical reality of the Elizabethan polity into the form of myth. The point is that for Sophocles, as for Shakespeare, tragic action is not invention. It is the acceptance of the limitation of invention as the condition for theatrical creation. In *Hamlet,* a *Trauerspiel* rises to the level of tragedy.

Walter Benjamin's Slothful, Pensive Melancholy

SOMETHING IS ROTTEN not just in the state of Denmark: rottenness pervades the totality of human endeavor without the essential but essentially unforeseeable redemptive power of the divine will. Lest it be forgotten, Hamlet is a student in Wittenberg (now called Lutherstadt Wittenberg), and at the beginning of the play his only wish is to return to the *fons et origo* of the Reformation, where Luther nailed his Ninety-Five Theses to the door of Schloss-Kirche in 1517. In fact, the only desire that Hamlet expresses in the play, namely, the only desire that is genuinely *his* and not that of the ghost, say, is to return to Wittenberg. Interestingly, we learn of this desire indirectly through Claudius's counterdesire,

> For your intent
> In going back to school in Wittenberg,
> It is most retrograde to our desire

What lies behind *Hamlet* is the reality of the Reformation. For Benjamin, Hamlet articulates the Lutheran philosophy of Wittenberg:

> What is a man,
> If his chief good and market of his time
> Be but to sleep and feed? A beast, no more

Men without God are beasts in a putrefying world. If this is the case, then it is perhaps not surprising that

Hamlet's worldview is one of pensive melancholy, where "Pensiveness is characteristic above all of the mournful."[9] Indeed, Hamlet derives no small perverse pleasure from observing that the world is a goodly prison "in which there are many confines, wards and dungeons." Thus, the tenacious self-absorption of the melancholic prince is not cut off from the world of things. On the contrary, the melancholic is loyal to that world, what Benjamin calls the *creaturely,* but it is a world of things that are no longer used. Rather they lie around unused and often useless as objects of contemplation. We can link this contemplative detachment to the baroque fascination with the ruin, the fragment, and the array of objects that seem to simply lie around in Spanish and Dutch still-life paintings. For the melancholic, the world is indeed present, but only as *nature morte.*

For Benjamin, Hamlet betrays not the ancient world of heroic action and fate but the world of knowledge—embracing only dead objects, a world absent of radiance, deprived of soul. Mourning is characterized by a chronic deepening of intention and a surfeit of intention over action. This yields an intense contemplation of the kind that we see in Hamlet:

> Pensiveness is characteristic above all of the mournful. On the road to the object—no: within the object itself—this intention progresses as slowly and solemnly as the processions of the rulers advance.[10]

Within the object itself, Hamlet's "obsequious sorrow" knows not "seems"—"nay, it is."

In *Trauerspiel,* the ever-indecisive prince is the paradigm of the melancholic man.[11] This melancholy finds expression in one of the seven deadly sins: *sloth.* More particularly, the listlessness and dullness of heart of the saturnine prince are manifestations of the state of *acedia,* a kind of depressive position that was common to ascetics and solitaries in the medieval world. As he is wont, Benjamin quotes a thirteenth-century source, where *acedia* is linked to *tracheit,* in modern German *Trägheit,* "slowness" or "inertia." It is the precise word that Freud uses to describe the experience of the death drive.

This sloth or lethargy is an expression of a world without "the faintest glimmer of any spiritualization," as if it must literally depict this cessation of movement, this strangulation of pneuma. Benjamin writes, "The whole of nature is personalized, not so as to be made *more* [emphasis ours] inward, but, on the contrary—so as to be deprived of soul."[12] The appearance of the perturbed spirit of Hamlet's father, trapped in a prison house between mortal and immortal life, finds its resonance here. In the end, it is perhaps no different for Hamlet's father than it is for Hamlet—they live, as noted by Stephen Greenblatt, in a medieval purgatory. Their melancholic tale is one that cannot but must be told, a story at the limits of what is human. If his father could "a tale unfold whose lightest word would harrow up thy soul, freeze thy young blood," then this "eternal blazon must not be to ears of flesh and blood." Hamlet also dies urging the ever-faithful Horatio not to die with him but to live to tell his tale:

> You that look pale and tremble at this chance,
> That are but mutes or audience to this act,
> Had I but time—as this fell sergeant, death,
> Is strict in his arrest—O, I could tell you—
> But let it be. Horatio, I am dead;

Thou livest. Report me and my cause aright
To the unsatisfied.

From the "must not be" of Hamlet Senior to the "let it be" of Hamlet himself—an uncanny repetition of the earlier "let be" of which we made much (indeed, the ghost adds "let me be")—father and son remain bound in silence, trembling on a certain threshold without redemption.

Others, perhaps Horatio, will speak. Here, however, matters must be qualified, for in his final two speeches in the play, Horatio only promises to speak of these "carnal, bloody and unnatural acts," delayed by Fortinbras's call to bear up Hamlet's dead body. We do not learn the tragical history of Hamlet from Horatio's mouth. We simply hear his intent to "truly deliver" that story, although the nature of that truth is unclear. Instead, we are confronted once again with the scene of a dead object, this time Hamlet's corpse—"the soldiers' music and the rites of war speak loudly for him," for "such a sight as this becomes the field, but here shows much amiss."

This loyalty to the world of things, the suffering of life, oddly, is also depicted by Benjamin as a turning to stone—a theme he finds recurring throughout German *Trauerspiel.* The mourner does not cry, crying does not soften his heart or wet the ground of the beloved, but like a stone, the mourner only sweats on the outside when the weather is damp. The mourner is pure surface, a mirror of external atmosphere.

Despite Hamlet's chatter, we have been arguing for a kind of silence maintained with regard to the question of truth that acts like a mute rock throughout the play. We'll come back to this silence, but let us recall

Hamlet's response to the second appearance of his father's ghost:

> On him, on him! Look you, how pale he glares!
> His form and cause conjoined, preaching to stones,
> Would make them capable.

The subject Hamlet is the object stone. Or in the words of Lear embracing the corpse of his daughter Cordelia: "Howl, howl, howl, howl! O, you are men of stones." What makes stones capable? What form and cause conjoined might preach to stones thus?

Hamlet is cold, earthly life itself in the midst of protest. Benjamin is quite moving on this point:

> For those who look deeper saw the scene of their existence as a rubbish heap of partial, inauthentic actions. Life itself protested against this. It feels deeply that it is not there to be devalued by faith. It is overcome by a deep horror at the idea that the whole of existence might proceed in such a way. The idea of death fills it with a profound terror. Mourning is the state of mind in which feeling revives the empty world in the form of a mask and derives an enigmatic satisfaction from contemplating it.[13]

Hamlet, Benjamin says, wants to die a hero's death—in one breath to take in both his death and his destiny, transforming his guilt into a point of honor—but cannot. Mourning, lethargy, sloth, ruin, deathly contemplation, and becoming stone are all that is left to him. The consequences of a life that proceeds only from within the object itself: a point that Benjamin radicalizes from Freud's "Mourning and Melancholia."

Is this not in fact a strange echo of Schmitt's mute rock of historical reality? Is not Hamlet himself, for

Benjamin, this mute rock erupting in the play in the form of mourning? For both thinkers there is no simple opposition between inside and outside. What is most inward and intimate in the play is depicted as a pure externality that breaks or intrudes into the play despite itself and that the play nonetheless increasingly moves toward. What mourning and historical reality share for both these thinkers is something on the level of facticity, force, and fate—something, as we've pointed out, that reads too close to the description of the Freudian drive to ignore, and that Lacan will go on to describe as the dimension of the Real. One smashes against and breaks upon this Real, or, to turn it around, one is broken into, subjected to, veritably raped by this excess. It is the traumatic encounter with alterity—"what dreams may come when we have shuffled off this mortal coil," the "dread of something after death." That Hamlet cannot face this force of fate, that he always flees it, means he is condemned to mirror it—silence, ruin, excess, stone. Put more simply: an obsessive contemplation of death in life, and life after death.

Is Hamlet *a Christian Tragedy?*

BENJAMIN MAKES a bewildering claim: there is Christian redemption in *Hamlet.* Hamlet's melancholic self-absorption, which seems so redolent of the atmosphere of German *Trauerspiel* and its melancholic *acedia,* where the divine light seems as weak as the Scandinavian winter sun, attains to a Christianity that is denied to *Trauerspiel.* For Benjamin, Hamlet's life, about which he endlessly ruminates in his soliloquies, "points, before its extinction, to the Christian providence in whose bosom his mournful images are transformed into a blessed existence." The textual basis for Benjamin's claim is Hamlet's speech where he talks about a "special providence in the fall of a sparrow." We suggested that this speech could as easily, or perhaps even more easily, bear an Epicurean rather than Christian gloss. Be that as it may, the claim is that Hamlet redeems his melancholy in an affirmation of providence. Benjamin writes, "only Shakespeare was capable of striking Christian sparks from the baroque rigidity of the melancholic."[14] Despite his melancholic self-absorption, Hamlet attains to Christianity.

Benjamin cites Hamlet's final words in support of his view, "The rest is silence." For Benjamin, as we saw above, silence is the *sublime* element in tragedy, the criterion for distinguishing ancient tragedy from modern

Trauerspiel. Benjamin sees *Hamlet* as a modern return to or even rebirth of the silence characteristic of ancient tragedy. Although this is a questionable interpretation of ancient tragedy, Benjamin's argument requires an even-greater suspension of disbelief. The claim is not that *Hamlet* is just a recovery of the sublimity of ancient tragedy—should such a thing be possible in any sense—it is the transfiguration of that sublimity from pagan antiquity to Christian modernity.[15]

So, is *Hamlet* a Christian tragedy? For a discussion of this precise point, we should return to Schmitt. In the second and final appendix to his book on *Hamlet,* intriguingly entitled "On the Barbaric Character of Shakespearean Drama," he criticizes Benjamin's *Trauerspiel* book. For Schmitt, very simply, "Shakespeare's drama is no longer Christian."[16] Benjamin risks transforming Hamlet, "into a kind of 'God's player' in the Lutheran sense." The justification for Benjamin's interpretation turns on the meaning of providence in the "fall of a sparrow" speech. Hamlet mentions *special* providence, which is a theological dogma that means the direct intervention of God in the world that breaks with natural law. This is opposed to *general* providence, which is God's continuous preservation of creation in accordance with natural law. The sense of Hamlet's words would seem to require a conception of general rather than special providence otherwise the fall of the sparrow would be something closer to the order of a miracle. Also, as Schmitt points out, matters might have been made easier if Shakespeare had simply alluded to Matthew 10:29, "Are not two sparrows sold for a farthing? And one of them shall not fall on the ground without your Father." But this, once again, implies general rather than special providence. The point is that there is theological confusion here, and to base a Christian interpretation of the play on Hamlet's mention of providence is peremptory, to say the least.

Do It, England

SCHMITT MAKES A second and mightily interesting criticism of Benjamin. As we saw above, Benjamin alludes directly to Schmitt's definition of sovereignty from *Political Theology* early in the *Trauerspiel* book, where the sovereign is the subject who decides on the state of exception. But—surprising perhaps—Schmitt begs to disagree with Benjamin's use of his conception of sovereignty because it fails to grasp the essential difference between England and Continental Europe. In short, Schmitt claims that Benjamin is too *Schmittian* in his understanding of the political.

The problem here is that Schmitt's conceptions of sovereignty and the political presuppose the existence of the modern state, specifically the European states like France, which replaced the medieval order of feudal castes and estates and sought to marginalize the role of the Catholic Church in political affairs. Schmitt's problem with applying his own conception of sovereignty to *Hamlet* is that England at the end of the sixteenth and beginning of the seventeenth century could in no way be described as a state. England was not political; it was *barbaric*.

Between the defeat of the Spanish Armada in 1588 and the so-called Glorious Revolution in 1688, England was indeed on its way to a form of statehood, but it was not the Continental model, which we might define as a *territorial* or *terrestrial* state. It was rather a *maritime* conception of the state, which did not need to pass through "the constricted passage of Continental statehood."[17] The emergent English state was not identified with land so much as sea. In the seventeenth century, beginning with pirates, privateers, and corsairs and moving into vast colonial trading companies, plantation slavery, and eventually the Industrial Revolution, England comes to define itself not through land but through "the maritime appropriation of the world's oceans."[18]

England deterritorialized itself. It turned barbarism and piracy into maritime trade and colonial expropriation. England became a kind of *thalassocracy*. In Continental political terms, England is an essentially eccentric state. It is a remarkable fact that the first production of *Hamlet* (for which there is a written record) was at sea, off the coast of present-day Sierra Leone. Having set sail, along with two other ships, from England for the East Indies in March 1607, Captain William Keeling of *The Red Dragon* reports that on September 5 of that year his crew "gave the tragedie of Hamlett." He reports a second performance on September 31 and notes that it kept "my people from idleness and unlawful games or sleepe." Of course, this raises tantalizing but unanswerable questions about the nature of the text that was employed by the crew, the popular capacity of a drama like *Hamlet* to be performed by a group of sailors, and the commercial and incipient colonial context for the whole event. But let us just note that the documented performance history of *Hamlet* begins at sea off the West African coast.

So, paradoxically, Benjamin's Schmittian conception of the political is unable to grasp two sets of distinctions that define the world of *Hamlet* according to Schmitt: the political versus the barbaric, and the territorial versus the maritime. Shakespearean drama moves between the poles of both these distinctions, which indeed give it the sense of having feet in both an older, barbaric world and the newer political world. Elizabethan drama, like its Attic predecessor, is stretched between a world that is passing away and one that is coming into being. But what is coming into being is not a state on the French model, defined by politics, police, and politesse. England became a looser, eccentric liberal state, more like a series of estates, defined by the traces of the barbaric and where politics passed through piracy.

Hamlet, of course, is saved by pirates and calls them "thieves of mercy." After the elaborately described and cunningly executed exchange of letters that saved Hamlet's life when he was at sea, both literally and metaphorically, the English ambassador somehow turns up onstage with Fortinbras at the end of the play to tell Hamlet that his commandment is fulfilled, and "Rosencrantz and Guildenstern are dead." Sometime earlier, dispatching Hamlet to his death, Claudius exclaimed, "Do it, England." Well, England did it, but not quite in the way that Claudius had intended.

England is identified with both political and behavioral eccentricity throughout *Hamlet.* As the Clown-Gravedigger says at the beginning of act 5, Hamlet was sent to England because he was mad, but "Twill not be seen in him there. There the men are as mad as he." And indeed, it is curious how often in this allegedly

Danish play with so many oddly Latinate, Italianized names (Claudius, Barnardo, Francisco, and Marcellus), the word "England" should appear. We counted at least twenty-one occasions. As with *The Merchant of Venice* and *The Tempest,* everything opens onto the sea.

Germany Is Hamlet,
and Hamlet Is Germany

THE IMPLIED QUESTION in the title of Schmitt's book—*Hamlet or Hecuba*—is rhetorical: we prefer Hamlet, of course. After all, what is Hecuba to us or are we to Hecuba? Schmitt's closing lines are revealing:

> Mary Stuart is still for us something other than Hecuba. Even the fate of the Atreidae does not affect us as deeply as that of the unhappy Stuarts. This royal line was shattered by the fate of the European religious schism. Out of its history grew the seed of the tragic myth of Hamlet.

As we suggested above, what lies behind *Hamlet* for Schmitt is the reality of the Reformation and the disintegration of Catholic Europe. As is well known, Schmitt was hardly a cheerleader for Protestantism. When Claudius asks Hamlet where he has hidden the corpse of Polonius, he replies:

> A certain convocation of politic worms are e'en at him. Your worm is your only emperor for diet.

Is it too much of a stretch to see this as an allusion to the anti-Lutheran Diet of Worms from 1521, with the suggestion of an analogy between the spidery body of Polonius/Corambis and the vast web of the Catholic Church? Perhaps. But Schmitt's claim is that religious schism and bloody conflict in England are the mute rock of historical reality refracted in *Hamlet,* through the fate of the unhappy Stuarts, and the source of genuine tragic action. Such a reality cannot be invented. Schmitt's point is that we still live (or at least he still lives) in the wake of the reality of religious schism and its political effects. This gives an added poignancy to Schmitt's citing of Ferdinand Freiligrath's poem, which is a leitmotif of the book, repeated in its final paragraph, "Germany is Hamlet! / Solemn and silent." The implication is that Germany has spent too long thinking and drinking in the taverns of Wittenberg.

One might reply that Hamlet was not German at all—au contraire, one might quip. But the appeal of *Hamlet* in the German context has to be understood with reference to what we said about the relation between the barbaric and the political. Shakespeare becomes that idealized imago through which nascent German identity was to be constructed in the passage from barbarism to a political state. To put it into the form of what Hegel would call a speculative proposition: *Germany is Hamlet, and Hamlet is Germany.* But if this is the statement of the problem—Germany suffers from Hamletization, and Hamlet suffers from a Lutheran Germanization—then how might this fault be addressed or even repaired?[19]

A Fault to Heaven

LONG MEDITATIONS on the flaw or defect in nature, indeed the question of original sin, haunt Hamlet. Finding fault (pun intended) precedes any question of redemption, transfiguration, or unification, an inheritance that we might mark as particularly Lutheran. However, the circular interchanges on the question of guilt and sin throughout *Hamlet* never arrive at any redemption against Benjamin's thin claim based on the mention of providence. Although Hamlet says, "My fate cries out" after his initial encounter with the ghost, it seems as if fault replaces fate, and finding fault—inside, outside, human, nature, or divine—becomes imperative.

In fact, the possibility (or impossibility) of reconciliation between fate and freedom pervades act 1, with the visitation of Hamlet's dead father's ghost that "bodes some strange eruption to our state." Horatio and Barnardo plead with the ghost to speak, imagining that their country's fate—caught in a dispute over territory beginning with a war between the elder Hamlet and Fortinbras—hangs in the balance of the ghost's appearance. But the ghost does not speak of country matters. Claudius, as the new king, seems to make light of the problems with Norway, instead concentrating his watch on Hamlet. From the mouth of the villain and hypocrite Claudius, Hamlet is named as at fault.

In words that ring empty though nonetheless true, Claudius accuses Hamlet of stubbornly holding on to grief over his dead father—a fault against heaven, the dead, and nature herself—injuring his position as most immediate to the throne:

> . . . but to persever
> In obstinate condolement is a course
> Of impious stubbornness, 'Tis unmanly grief,
> It shows a will most incorrect to heaven,
> A heart unfortified, a mind impatient,
> An understanding simple and unschooled;
> For what we know must be, and is, as common
> As any the most vulgar thing to sense—
> Why should we in our peevish opposition
> Take it to heart? Fie, 'tis a fault to heaven,
> A fault against the dead, a fault to nature,
> To reason most absurd, whose common theme
> Is death of fathers, and who still hath cried
> From the first corpse till he that died today
> "This must be so." We pray you throw to earth
> This unprevailing woe.

To sum up and update Claudius's speech: *it is what it is.* Hamlet does not accept what is, nor does he answer Claudius. Instead, he pledges his allegiance to his mother. As the court empties, we hear Hamlet's first soliloquy wherein he oscillates between a fault located either in nature, which "grows to seed, things rank and gross in nature/Possess it merely," or in his mother, "a beast that wants discourse of reason/Would have mourned longer."

At the sight of the postconnubial drunken celebrations, Hamlet again lapses into a meditation on flaw and original sin, saying to Horatio:

That, for some vicious mole of nature in them,
As in their birth wherein they are not guilty
(Since nature cannot choose his origin),
By their o'ergrowth of some complexion
Oft breaking down the pales and forts of reason,
Or by some habit that too much o'erleavens
The form of plausive manners—that these men,
Carrying, I say, the stamp of one defect
(Being Nature's livery or Fortune's star),
His virtues else, be they as pure as grace,
As infinite as man may undergo,
Shall in the general censure take corruption
From that particular fault: the dram of eale
Doth all the noble substance of a doubt,
To his own scandal.

There is a vicious mole in nature that corrupts men from birth: a stain, a vice that breaks with reason and becomes the overgrown force of corrupt habit.[20] This defect—even if only "the stamp of one defect"—throws into doubt any nobility of substance. With these words said, man is condemned to a fallen state, the ghost of Hamlet's father suddenly appears, who is also described as "old mole." While we all know the famous line of Marcellus, "Something is rotten in the state of Denmark," what follows seems even more apt. Horatio's rejoinder, "Heaven will direct it," is met with Marcellus's curt "Nay."

What the ghost speaks about is in fact his own plea for Catholic absolution. Cut off in the blossom of his sin, no reckoning made, "Unhouseled, disappointed, unaneled," sent to his account with his imperfections on his head —"O horrible, O horrible, most horrible!"— Hamlet Senior is doomed for a certain time to walk the night and in the day fast in fires till his foul crimes are purged away. One has to die at the right time, in the right way, reconciled with God before facing one's fate. While this seems to put the cart before the horse, are we not all then left praying for a Catholic Shakespeare?

Unbearable Contingency—
Hegel's Hamlet

HEGEL IS *the* philosopher of the tragic. He is the philosopher with the deepest understanding of the nature of tragedy: its internal movement, contradictions, and collisions, indeed what we might call the *collisional* character of tragedy. If that manner of conceiving experience that Hegel calls dialectics can be understood as thinking in movement, then it is arguable that dialectics has its genesis in tragedy or at least in a certain understanding of tragedy. Although it might be said that other thinkers—like Schelling, his erstwhile roommate—also see tragedy dialectically, the vital difference between them and Hegel turns on the question of *history.* Any philosophical idealization of tragedy that lacks a historical understanding of art's unfolding is empty formalism. As Benjamin notes, what he calls "the philosophy of tragedy" is a "theory of the moral order of the world, without any reference to historical content, in a system of generalized sentiments."[21]

What is misguided in the multiple iterations of "the philosophy of tragedy" is its universalistic ahistoricism, usually based on a series of metaphysical assumptions about a purported human nature.

For Hegel, and this is already clear from his reading of *Antigone* in the *Phenomenology of Spirit* onward, tragedy is the aesthetic articulation of the historical disintegration of ethical life, or *Sittlichkeit,* through the strife of civil war and the life-and-death struggle between the essential elements of the political life of the city-state. In tragedy, the substance of ethical life divides against itself, dissolving in war and splitting into a multitude of separate individual atoms. This passes over into the impotent Stoicism of the solitary self in a world defined by law—that is, Rome—and the experience of modern self-alienation that Hegel associates with the word *Kultur.* History must form an essential part of any account of tragedy. This is where we may rejoin *Hamlet.*

Moving (not unproblematically, it must be acknowledged) from the early Hegel of the *Phenomenology* to the late Hegel of the *Aesthetics*—and indeed the 1,300 pages of the *Aesthetics* conclude and culminate with a stunning interpretation of *Hamlet*—in modern tragedy individuals do not act for the sake of the substance of ethical life. What presses for satisfaction, rather, is the subjectivity of their private character. In ancient tragedy, the conflict at the heart of the substance of ethical life finds expression in opposed but equally justified characters, each of whom embodies a clear pathos: Antigone versus Creon, or Orestes versus Clytemnestra. However, if conflict in ancient tragedy finds articulation in the externality of substance, then in modern tragedy the conflict is internal to subjectivity.

Hegel asserts that in the portrayal of individual characters Shakespeare stands "at an almost unapproachable height," making his creations "free artists of their own selves."[22] As such, Shakespeare's tragic characters are "real, directly living, extremely varied" and possessing a "sublimity and striking power of expression." Yet—and here comes the dialectical underside of this claim—creatures like Hamlet lack any resolution and capacity for decision. They are dithering figures in the grip of "a twofold passion which drives them from one decision or one deed to another simultaneously." In other words, as in Schmitt, they are Hamletized, vacillating characters inwardly divided against themselves. Upheld only by the force of their conflicted subjectivity, characters like Hamlet or Lear either plunge blindly onward or allow themselves to be lured to their avenging deed by external circumstances, led along, that is, by contingency.

In the vast sweep of an ancient dramatic trilogy, like the *Oresteia*, what is at stake in the *agon*, or dramatic conflict, is eternal justice shaped by the power of fate, which saves the substance of the ethical life of the city against individuals, like Orestes and Clytemnestra, who were becoming too independent and colliding violently with each other. Hegel insists, and we think he is right, that if a similar justice appears in modern tragedy, then it is more like *criminal* justice, where—as with Macbeth or with Lear's daughters—a wrong has been committed and the protagonists deserve the nasty demise that's coming to them. Tragic denouement in Shakespearean tragedy is not the rigorous working out of fate, but "purely the effect of unfortunate circumstances and external accidents which might have turned out otherwise and produced a happy ending."[23] Hegel enjoyed a happy ending, as we will see presently, but the point is that the modern individual must endure the contingency and fragility of "all that is mundane and must endure the fate of finitude."

Here Hegel's remarks on *Hamlet* begin to cut much deeper—the problem is that we cannot *bear* this contingency. Hegel argues that:

> We feel a pressing demand for a necessary correspon-
> dence between the external circumstances and what
> the inner nature of those fine characters really is.[24]

Thus, we want Hamlet's death not simply to be the effect of chance, owing to the accidental switch of poisoned rapiers. *The Tragicall Historie of Hamlet, Prince of Denmarke* affects its audience profoundly, and it seems that there is a deep need—at once aesthetic and moral—for something greater than mere accident. It is as if there is something unbearable about the contingency of life that finds articulation in *Hamlet* and elsewhere in Shakespeare. This is what leads, we think, to Benjamin's claim that *Hamlet* is a Christian tragedy of providence or indeed the nostalgic memory of that Christian longing in Schmitt. It is the yearning for a redemptive artwork that would both reveal our modern, alienated condition and heal it. It is a nostalgic yearning for reconciliation between the individual and the cosmic order that one finds all over Shakespeare criticism.

Such nostalgia is indeed one way of interpreting the character of Hamlet, bound by a longing that is his very paralysis. From his warped idealization of his father as a lost Hyperion who offers one assurance of a man, to his dream of a perfected act that does not overstep the modesty of nature and strikes at the exactly right time, to his overblown rage centered on the thought of multifarious villains—"O villain, villain, smiling, damnèd villain!" "That one may smile, and smile, and be a villain"—Hamlet might be seen as a conservative rebel against the contingency and atomized anomie of the new social order. And, not to belabor the Freudian points (enough of that is on the way), his chief complaints center on the figures of his Oedipal triangle—himself, his mother, and Claudius—with the dead father propped up as all that is right in a world gone to hell. Perhaps it is this yearning for a Catholic Shakespeare that must be given up in order to see *Hamlet* aright and see ourselves in its light. Perhaps we will have to dispense with the ghost's prayer for an unadulterated life, for Catholic absolution, for an absolute.

Hegel Likes a Happy Ending

HEGEL DOESN'T PUT it as strongly as this, and, in any case, he has a dialectical trump card up his sleeve: tragedy is overcome by comedy, and both are overcome by philosophy. The failure of aesthetic reconciliation leads to the requirement for philosophical reconciliation. For Hegel, not without some nostalgia for the loss of Greek ethical life and his deep admiration for Sophocles, comedy supplants tragedy, and comedy is the very element in which art dissolves and prepares the passage for conceptual elaboration, namely philosophy. Comedy—and one thinks of Aristophanes, whom Hegel constantly praises, as well as Shakespeare's comedies and also of Hegel's wonderful reading of Diderot's *Rameau's Nephew* in the *Phenomenology of Spirit*—is the raising of art to the level of cognition where it then dissolves. Hegel's system is a comedy and has to be a comedy, insofar as history culminates with the institutional expression of freedom in the form of the modern state. Funny. This is where we could begin a metacritique of Hegel, along the lines one can find in the very young Marx.[25] But the aesthetic point is that perhaps Hegel will always have the last laugh, that comedy stands higher than tragedy, and that the true comédie humaine is philosophy.

This is why Hegel likes a happy ending. He makes the brilliant remark that might echo in the ears of contemporary partisans of trauma, loss, and generalized aesthetic miserabilism:

> I must admit that for my part a happy denoucment is to be preferred. And why not? To prefer misfortune just because it is misfortune, instead of a happy resolution, has no other basis but a superior sentimentality which indulges in grief and suffering and finds more interest in them than in the painless situations that it regards as commonplace.[26]

The tragedy of suffering, such as we find in Sophocles, is only ethically justified when it serves some higher outlook, such as fate, otherwise it is simply an Eeyore-esque wallowing in misery (which, incidentally, makes Hegel closer to Winnie the Pooh). A happy ending would be better. If art—and Hegel is thinking in particular of Greek statuary—is the unity of the idea and appearance in sensuous ideality, then comedy can only present this unity as self-destruction. For Hegel, the absolute can no longer be contained within aesthetic form. Comedy is art's dissolution and its passage beyond itself. This is why comedy is the entrance into philosophy.

And of course the turn from comedy toward philosophy, out from one's being-as-misery-guts, is already foreshadowed by Hamlet. After the encounter with the ghost, Hamlet cautions Horatio, "There are more things in heaven and earth, Horatio, / Than are dreamt of in your philosophy," and then promptly (and weirdly, we might add) tells him that his plan is to put on an antic disposition. The next time we hear from Hamlet, he is the clownish provocateur in the fishmonger scene with Polonius, followed by the Hamlet of satirical philosophical sparring with Rosencrantz and Guildenstern.

The oscillation between tragicomedy and philosophy is an imbroglio best summed up by Hamlet himself as he hurtles toward the limits of rationality:

> HAMLET: O God, I could be bounded in a nut shell and count myself a king of infinite space, were it not that I have bad dreams.
> GUILDENSTERN: Which dreams indeed are ambition, for the very substance of the ambitious is merely the shadow of a dream.
> HAMLET: A dream itself is but a shadow.
> ROSENCRANTZ: Truly, and I hold ambition of so airy and light a quality that it is but a shadow's shadow.
> HAMLET: Then are our beggars bodies, and our monarchs and outstretched heroes but the beggars' shadows.—Shall we to court? for, by my fay, I cannot reason.

Who else other than Hegel could follow Hamlet's reasoning here, whereby substance dialectically reverses into shadow, infinite space is a bad dream, ambition is a ghost that takes flight in sleep, and a monarch is found only in the shade of a beggar's body. Hamlet's self-consciousness is the Hegelian prowess of the tautological infinity of a nutshell—an identity that is its own undoing. What aesthetic reconciliation can there be? Perhaps this helps explain T. S. Eliot's statement that Hamlet is an artistic failure, along with his scathing critique that the longing for creative power in the minds of critics has led to a particular weakness where instead of studying a work of art they find only their semblable. Goethe sees Hamlet as Goethe, and Coleridge sees Hamlet as Coleridge. To be clear, we do not see any aspects of ourselves or each other in Hamlet.

Hamlet Is a Lost Man

THE FINAL SCENE of *Hamlet*, like the final scene of *King Lear*, is not the triumph of some Christian idea of providence nor is it any rebirth of Attic tragedy. It is simply a stage full of corpses, what Adorno perspicuously sees as a crowd of puppets on a string after a killing spree, and what James Joyce sees, in an eerily prophetic remark, "The bloodboltered shambles in act five is a forecast of the concentration camp." In other words, *Hamlet* is a *Trauerspiel* whose force is tragicomic and whose macabre ending verges on the melodramatic. As Melville writes of Hamlet in *Pierre; or, The Ambiguities*, he falls "dabbling in the vomit of his loathed identity."

But there is one further and fascinating twist in the tail of Hegel's reading of *Hamlet*. Looked at from the outside, Hamlet's death might seem to be accidentally caused by the unfortunate switcheroo of swords. But on two occasions, Hegel advances a brief but perceptive psychological profile of the Danish prince. What he finds inside Hamlet is morbidity, melancholy, worry, weakness, and, most of all, in a word repeated three times in these passages, *disgust.* Hegel writes:

> But death lay from the beginning in the background of Hamlet's mind. The sands of time do not content him. In his melancholy and weakness, his worry, his disgust at all the affairs of life, we sense from

the start that in all his terrible surroundings he is a lost man, almost consumed by inner disgust before death comes to him from outside.[27]

Hamlet is a lost man. He is the wrong man. He should never have been commanded by the ghost to avenge his murder. His disgust with the world induces not action but *acedia,* a slothful lethargy. Hamlet just lacks the energy. As Hegel writes:

> His noble soul was not made for this kind of ener-
> getic activity; and, full of disgust with the world
> and life, what with decision, proof, arrangements
> for carrying out his resolve, and being bandied from
> pillar to post, he eventually perishes owing to his
> own hesitation and a complication of external cir-
> cumstances.[28]

It is our contention that what is caught sight of by Hegel is a Hamlet Doctrine that turns on the corrosive dialectic of knowledge and action, where the former disables the latter and insight into the truth induces a disgust with existence. He cannot, or will not, imagine anything more in the gap that opens up. Rubbernecking the chaos and wreckage of the world that surround him while chattering and punning endlessly, Hamlet finally finds himself fatally struck and strikes out impetuously, asking Horatio to sing him a lullaby. What is so heroic about Hamlet's disgust? Do we even *like* him?

Part II

Hamletizing Psychoanalysis

To approach *Hamlet* psychoanalytically is not simply to psychoanalyze the play's eponymous hero. It is not a question of putting Hamlet on the couch, which in any case would be weirdly anachronistic, but rather to hear something in *Hamlet* that allows us to put psychoanalysis on the couch and to the test. The mad trajectory of the play holds a message for the psychoanalyst, not vice versa. We do not need a theory of sexuality to understand the play; we need the play to tell us about sexuality. Give Hamlet a little more credit than this, dear psychoanalysts! Hamlet's powerful reflexivity, like a patient's, will always be ten steps ahead of any banal game of interpretation. It takes a different act of reading, something other than this game of scholarship and interpretation, to get inside the play. Isn't this already mirrored in Hamlet's relations with the bumbling adviser and self-appointed diagnostician, Polonius? Our conviction is that what is staged in *Hamlet* touches very close to the experience of being a psychoanalyst, that is, someone who has to listen to patients day after day, hour after hour. If we cup our ear, then we may hear something in *Hamlet* that allows us to become oriented to whatever might be meant by the idea of psychoanalytic cure.

The causal reversal implied here is not a natural one for psychoanalysis and is a general problem with its applied version, limping after scholarship that better understands the nature of aesthetic form.[1] Since Freud linked Hamlet and Oedipus in *The Interpretation of Dreams,* the claim of psychoanalysts has often been that they have finally solved Hamlet's mystery—the mystery of his inhibition, the mystery of the disjunction between plot and character, and the mystery of the play's success. Stripper of the Veil of Isis, with the true answer to the Sphinx's riddle, the Oedipus complex provides the definitive interpretation of *Hamlet.* As Freud writes with delightfully arrogant assertion from a short text unpublished in his lifetime, "The conflict of *Hamlet* is so effectively concealed that it was left to me to unearth it."[2]

Freud was weirdly obsessed with the historical theory that Shakespeare was Edward de Vere, the seventeenth Earl of Oxford. He pestered Ernest Jones (the great biographer of Freud who wrote *Hamlet and Oedipus* at Freud's urging) to investigate the claim, spoke on the Earl of Oxford theory in his acceptance speech for the Goethe Prize in 1930, and wrote about it in *Moses and Monotheism* and *An Outline of Psychoanalysis,* both written in the final years of his life.[3] Freud also believed that something in Shakespeare's life, like the death of his father in 1601 or the death of his only son, Hamnet, or Hamlet, in 1596, must have stirred his unconscious in a way that forced him to write something as extraordinary as *Hamlet.* This led Freud down the path of a wild-goose chase for the "real" Shakespeare, essentially failing to see the facile character of this equivalence, irrespective of whether it is right or wrong (and while we are skeptical, it is still a theory that many believe).[4] Schmitt surpasses Freud in this respect, for at the very least he situates his "historical figure," James I of

England, in a wider sociohistorical context. For Freud it is simply a matter of finding the biographical proof that connects the dots in the way he wants.

Why do we feel the need to pin art to biography? Why engage in what Joyce rightly satirized as "Hamlet is Shakespeare or James 1 or Essex. Clergymen's discussions of the historicity of Jesus"? Isn't there so much more to be said about the play than this? Psychoanalysis always looks like a terrible parody of itself at these moments and still fails today to escape this problem when it pronounces upon culture like a predictable grid that can be laid atop anything and everything. We'd like to believe that Freud is more interesting than this, indeed he is, but when it comes to applied psychoanalysis, especially with respect to Shakespeare, it is hard to escape the conclusion that he was culpable of this form of interpretation. Hamlet, the alleged archetype of modern, inward man, is an apt target in a vogue for psychologization that begins in the nineteenth century, what the jeremiad-writing Freud scholar Philip Rieff sardonically called "the triumph of the therapeutic"—and today nothing is more therapeutic than a healthy dose of Shakespeare.

Psychoanalysis itself, its clinical practice, as *we* understand it, really has very little to do with this. So it is Lacan's work with *Hamlet*—including his ever-present general disdain for decades of truly bad work by psychoanalysts on aesthetics (and on everything else for that matter)—that appeals to us as something different. He was deeply embedded in surrealism and philosophy and was part of an effort that reinvented the question of criticism. Like Shakespeare, Lacan knows something powerful about the poetic theatricality of language, which will always supersede any supposed historical reality. He sees the necessity of playing with the veil of illusion that makes action possible, his way of redefining Freud's notion of sublimation. We hope to demonstrate the intricacy of Lacan's work with the play, including how he works to reinterpret and push Freud past his reading of *Hamlet*.[5] Truth does not come from the past but from the future, meaning that what matters is not proof or any supposed veracity but what is said and how in an act that cuts through the past. Interpretation is revelation.

Lacan engages in this reading of *Hamlet* in his 1958–59 seminar "Desire and Its Interpretation."[6] This was the sixth year of his seminar, which lasted for some twenty-eight years.[7] So if Freud couples Oedipus and Hamlet reading forward, where the Danish prince confirms the newly minted Oedipus complex, then Lacan is coupling Hamlet and Antigone, reading backward. Lacan's reading of *Hamlet* develops the question about the formations of the unconscious and presages his remarks on sublimation, the relation of the beautiful to the good, and the ethics of desire in his reading of *Antigone*. Antigone is the secret future of Oedipus and Hamlet.

It is important to see Hamlet as Antigone's tragic counterpart. Where he ends, she begins—literally, as someone marked and destined for death. For Lacan, Antigone is an emblem of femininity, while Hamlet would seem to have an absolute horror of it. This is seen most clearly in his violence against Ophelia and his mother. Antigone, in her grief, Lacan says, is completely faithful to her singular and irreplaceable object of love—"I will never have another brother," she insists—and to her desire to bury him. Hamlet is bereft of his desire, cannot act, and all the objects that surround him are degraded and rendered fungible: women are whores; stepfathers are liars; mothers are criminals; the world is rotten and putrefying. While Antigone deftly defies Creon's laws, claiming that she follows an inner divine call, Hamlet waffles and prates, unable to find a belief in anything beyond.

Thus, Lacan inverts the original Freudian pairing of Oedipus and Hamlet and, in so doing, enacts a small but significant displacement between Oedipus and Antigone, advancing the figure of a woman instead of man. Antigone is described in Sophocles's play as a manly woman who doesn't respect the time-honored Greek gender hierarchies. Hamlet's grief is also declared unmanly by Claudius in the first familial scene in the play. A relationship to desire, even in its negation as grief, seems to elicit an external complaint about the stability of gender identity. Hamlet and Antigone, taken together, tell us something about the action and aim of psychoanalysis—especially the precarious crossing of desire and gender that requires a kind of transgression of the law. Lacan's insistence on a "return to Freud" meant going back over the ground out of which the Oedipus complex sprang and from which psychoanalysis always seeks to find its bearings.

So let us return to Freud and the original moment at which Freud inaugurates the Oedipus complex in *The Interpretation of Dreams*. It is also where he first mentions *Hamlet*. The Danish prince is very much present at the birth of psychoanalysis.

Rebecca, Take Off Your Gown—
Freud and Fliess

IN CHAPTER 5 of *The Interpretation of Dreams,* in the section entitled "Dreams of the Death of Persons of Whom the Dreamer Is Fond," Freud smuggles in the Oedipus complex and engages in an infamous discussion of *Hamlet.* But this argument is—as so many of the key dreams in this book that form the nexus of Freud's self-analysis—presaged in letters between himself and his quasi-analyst Wilhelm Fliess. While Freud will always be the first analyst, the unmoved mover, there is the haunting story of Fliess as the unwitting psychoanalyst of Freud.

We know the story between Freud and Fliess one-sidedly, since we only have one-half of the correspondence. Freud burned the letters he received from Fliess and then sent his rich patroness and patient, Princess Marie Bonaparte, to buy his letters back from Fliess's widow. Once she had purchased them, she stubbornly refused to destroy them, seeing how "precious" they were to the story of the origin of psychoanalysis. Nevertheless, the letters were only published in full in 1985, suppressed by his psychoanalyst daughter, Anna, who took up her father's reign after his death in 1939.

In a key letter to Fliess on September 21, 1897, Freud criticizes his original theory of the traumatic sexual etiology of hysteria, a move that would steer him toward the "universality" of the Oedipus complex. Freud is beginning to come out of a period of despair and depression, trying to hold his doubts about his theories up to the challenge of judgment, in particular his seduction theory. If one does not rely on a theory of sexual trauma, then sexuality becomes a trope of the unconscious in the question of neurosis. This would make him the laughingstock of the medical profession. And yet, Freud perseveres. His self-analysis becomes critical in that he must find these wishes, the place of sexual fantasy, in himself. He writes:

> If I were depressed, confused, exhausted, such doubts would surely have to be interpreted as signs of weakness. Since I am in an opposite state, I must recognize them as the result of honest and vigorous intellectual work and must be proud that after going so deep I am still capable of such criticism. Can it be that this doubt merely represents an episode in the advance toward further insight? . . . Now to continue my letter. I vary Hamlet's saying, "To be in readiness": to be cheerful is everything! I could indeed feel quite discontent. The expectation of eternal fame was so beautiful, as was that of certain wealth, complete independence, travels, and lifting the children above the severe worries that robbed me of my youth. Everything depended upon whether or not hysteria would come out right. Now I can once again remain quiet and modest, go on worrying and saving. A little story from my collection occurs to me: "Rebecca, take off your gown; you are no longer a bride."

The last line is fascinating, "Rebecca, take off your gown; you are no longer a bride." Freud addresses himself to Fliess as a disappointed bride after the honeymoon is over. His expectations must be given up—his wishes for fame, wealth, and security—to be "in readiness." The great shift in psychoanalysis happens not because Freud the doctor finds the diagnostic criteria for the illness neurosis—"whether or not hysteria would come out right"—but because, having instead identified with his hysterical patients' pernicious dissatisfaction, finding the hysteric Hamlet in himself, he is closer to something more universal: the unconscious, the meaning of dreams, the tie between sexuality, repression, and symptoms, and of course the Oedipus complex. Freud, abandoned, abandons his own seduction theory, something that is still a source of great controversy.[8] Neurotics were not neurotic because they were seduced but because they wanted to be seduced or to seduce themselves. Freud is more modest and calm, "in readiness," having come close to his own unconscious fantasy.

He will take up Hamlet again in a letter a few weeks later where he announces his Oedipus-Hamlet theory to Fliess. On October 15, 1897, after elucidating his thoughts on Sophocles, he turns to Shakespeare:

> Fleetingly the thought passed through my head that the same thing might be at the bottom of *Hamlet* as well. I am not thinking of Shakespeare's conscious intention, but believe, rather, that a real event stimulated the poet to his representation, in that his unconscious understood the unconscious of his hero. How does Hamlet the hysteric justify his words, "Thus conscience does make cowards of us all"? How does he explain his irresolution in avenging his father by the murder of his uncle—the same man who sends his courtiers to their death without a scruple and who is positively precipitate in murder-

ing Laertes? How better than through the torment he suffers from the obscure memory that he himself had contemplated the same deed against his father out of passion for his mother, and—"use every man after his desert, and who should 'scape whipping?" His conscience is his unconscious sense of guilt. And is not his sexual alienation in his conversation with Ophelia typically hysterical? And his rejection of the instinct that seeks to beget children? And, finally, his transferral of the deed from his own father to Ophelia's? And does he not in the end, in the same marvelous way as my hysterical patients, bring down punishment on himself by suffering the same fate as his father of being poisoned by the same rival?

Freud's excitement in this letter is palpable, and while the formal publication of the Hamlet theory in the book on dreams a few years later looks more like a psychoanalysis of the Danish prince, here the inflection is on what *Hamlet* has to teach psychoanalysis, indeed what it was teaching Freud, struggling with his theory in its infancy. The original hysteric is Hamlet, who suffers from an obscure memory, "suffers mainly from reminiscences." Hamlet suffers from unknown repressed wishes both incestuous and rivalrous. Split off in this fashion, Hamlet, guilty, cannot but bring down punishment upon himself—the same punishment as his father whose murder he cannot avenge because *he* had wished for it at one time in the past. Hamlet is no better than the sinner whom he is to punish. His wishes are fundamentally transgressive.

On November 5, 1897, Freud anxiously writes to Fliess, dismayed by his lack of response to what he sees as an unheralded explanation of Hamlet's inaction:

You said nothing about my interpretation of *Oedipus Rex* and *Hamlet.* Since I have not told it to anyone else, because I can well imagine in advance the bewildered rejection, I should like to have a short comment on it from you.

One could speculate as to why Fliess seems unable to comment on Freud's Hamlet theory or to follow suit on his asking for approval or rejection. Perhaps it is all too close to the fierce competition and homoerotic passion between these two men, only thinly veiled by their quasi-paternalistic collegial exchange. But we need not speculate . . . the story unfolds. Written between 1887 and 1904, the letters terminate on a bitter note. In one version, the story ends with Freud—his new child, psychoanalysis, in hand—venturing off without Fliess and their sick symbiotic system of top-down approval. The son needs to kill his bad paranoiac father-analyst. In another version, Freud uses Fliess as a prop for low self-esteem while minting his controversial theories, steals from Fliess the importance of bisexuality, only then to discard him as useless once he achieves moderate fame and recognition. Either way, Freud kills off Fliess.

That Freud could not make the same critical moves with aggression and rivalry that he made with sexuality—displacing sexuality away from any supposed reality, metaphorizing its place between soma and psyche in terms of desire, drive, and wish—lingers in this story of his relation with Fliess. To understand the violence at the heart of *Hamlet,* we will have to wait for Lacan. Nevertheless, through these early successes and failures in the act of theorizing, filtered through Freud's self-analysis, one can see the act of founding psychoanalysis, an act that takes place in a curious identification with the traits of Hamlet's desire. A French analyst remarked that one could think of Freud as having had two analysts, Shakespeare and Fliess, one William hiding behind the other.[9] So while the Oedipus complex is hidden in a seemingly innocuous section on "typical dreams," something more is at stake—indeed, the very cornerstone of psychoanalysis itself.

I Have Bad Dreams

FREUD BEGINS THE section in *The Interpretation of Dreams* on Oedipus and Hamlet saying that there seem to be two kinds of dreams in this category of dreams of the death of loved ones: the first are dreams where there is no affect, one awakes feeling no grief for the death scene that had played out before one's eyes; the second, on the other hand, arouses intense affect, where one might even awake from sleep weeping bitterly. The first kind of dream, Freud suggests, usually has nothing to do with the death of the person in the dream, and analysis reveals that there is some other more salient content at stake. The second kind—the affect-laden dreams—are about the death of the loved one, precisely in terms of a death wish, a wish that the person in question may die. This is, Freud adds, not a current wish, but one that had existed at some much earlier time. In this second kind of dream, the example of sibling rivals is often paramount, the discussion of which finally leads Freud to the notion of a displaced wish for the death of parents. According to Freud, as is well known, we all harbor murderous and sexual wishes toward our parents.

Freud writes:

> *Oedipus Rex* is what is known as a tragedy of destiny. Its tragic effect is said to lie in the contrast between

the supreme will of the gods and the vain attempts of mankind to escape the evil that threatens them. The lesson which, it is said, the deeply moved spectator should learn from the tragedy is submission to the divine will and realization of his own impotence.

Freud continues:

[Oedipus's] destiny moves us only because it might have been ours—because the oracle laid the same curse upon us before our birth as upon him. It is the fate of all of us, perhaps, to direct our first sexual impulse towards our mother and our first hatred and our first murderous wish against our father. Our dreams convince us that this is so.

Oedipus, he claims, moves a modern audience as much as an ancient one because through the tragedy we gain access to the repressed wishes of childhood. More than this, Freud says, it

[s]trikes as a warning at ourselves and our pride, at us who since our childhood have grown so wise and so mighty in our own eyes. Like Oedipus, we live in ignorance of these wishes, repugnant to morality, which have been forced upon us by Nature, and after their revelation we may all of us well seek to close our eyes to the scenes of our childhood.[10]

Freud concludes that the attempt to harmonize divine omnipotence with human responsibility must fail in the subject matter of tragedy as with any other. This emphasis on failure is worth noting, especially with respect to pride and the vain attempts of mankind to overcome fate. For Freud, we close our eyes to our own origins and foolishly believe in our own omnipotence. Freud then immediately moves on to *Hamlet,* and what he has to say is very brief, just a few paragraphs.

Hamlet, Freud says, can do anything but punish the man who has killed his father and taken his place with his mother—in other words, the man who has done what he wished to do as a child. What we find instead is that the reproaches against Claudius are turned into self-reproaches, which remind him that he is literally no better than his murdering stepfather. Freud adds that a bitter distaste for sexuality erupts in his relations with Ophelia:

> In Oedipus the child's wishful fantasy . . . is brought into the open and realized as it would be in a dream. In Hamlet it remains repressed; and—just as in the case of a neurosis—we only learn of its existence from its inhibiting consequences.[11]

Hamlet shows us the inhibiting consequences in character of the repression of the Oedipus complex. While many have argued other reasons for Hamlet's inaction—lack of willpower, oversensitiveness, or a shortage of proof on Claudius's guilt—none of these seem to offer a substantial route of interpretation, split between objective and subjective reasoning. The enigma of the enigma of Hamlet is for Freud only more evidence for his theory, in other words, evidence of repression, a division within consciousness that expresses itself in this division within criticism. Hamlet is *the* neurotic subject par excellence.

Freud, at the end of the section on the analysis of absurd dreams, turns back again to *Hamlet*—his final remark on the play in *The Interpretation of Dreams.* He says:

> Dreams, then, are often most profound when they seem most crazy. In every epoch of history those who have had something to say but could not say it

without peril have eagerly assumed a fool's cap. The audience at whom their forbidden speech was aimed tolerated it more easily if they could at the same time laugh and flatter themselves with the reflection that the unwelcome words were clearly nonsensical. The Prince in the play, who had to disguise himself as a madman, was behaving just as dreams do in reality; so that we can say of dreams what Hamlet said of himself, concealing the true circumstances under a cloak of wit and unintelligibility: "I am but mad north-north-west: when the wind is southerly, I know a hawk from a hand-saw."[12]

A dream becomes absurd if it is faced with representing criticism or derision that, having been felt to be dangerous as such, has been repressed: an uncanny blind spot that haunts rationality. Perhaps this follows Margreta de Grazia's main thesis that Hamlet is enraged at his uncle and mother not on behalf of his father's murder but because *his* crown and *his* right to the throne have been usurped. This criticism is not only selfish, it is high treason, his uncle being king. The unconscious is a source of political insurrection.

Hamlet's very person is by necessity a wolf in sheep's clothing. His madness is only a seeming cover, "an antic disposition," strangely couched in the language of weather. "I am but mad north-north-west," to which his mother will reply in kind that he is "Mad as the sea and wind." Disguise is a powerful means, as Freud points out, of cloaking a judgment that cannot be revealed in its full weight—perhaps even to oneself. What is most true and profound, what demands our most forthright judgment and speech, often appears first in the form of nonsense, foolishness, and absurdity—in other words, through the logic of dreams. As Adorno said with his characteristic pomp, "in psychoanalysis, nothing is true except the exaggerations."

So for Freud, we do not understand because we do not know our own thoughts, memories, or intentions. *Hamlet*—like its audience—is about the exposure to the mystery of the human psyche, the mystery of desire. Whether he is up to the task to know what is in his own heart is the question that Freud was also asking himself simultaneous to this analysis, in particular concerning an inhibition around work and travel that had followed him up to his forty-fourth year of life. *The Interpretation of Dreams* could only be written concurrent with the first act of self-analysis, and this self-analysis turns on Freud's identification with the figure of Hamlet.

Psychoanalysts Eat Their Young

THE STORY OF OEDIPUS is not only parricidal; it is infanticidal. Oedipus's crimes are paid for by his children, his two sons, Polynices and Eteocles, caught in a fight to the death for their father's crown, having been set up in an impossible profession as rotating rulers. The psychoanalytic institution, as it played out after Freud, is also the story of what it means to be caught on this switchboard between parricide and infanticide—an unmitigated death drive, or better a death wish, transmitted through the generations. Like Kronos who kills his father and then fears being overthrown by his own children, eating every one of them at birth, psychoanalysis swallows its young in an orgy of death that can only be called befitting. Those children that wriggle free from the tyrannical grasp of their father return with a vengeance—with his same vengeance. How many sons did you swallow, Freud? And how many of those are now trying to kill you in effigy? Never has life so imitated art as it has with psychoanalysis playing out Freud's strange myth of the murder of the primal father in *Totem and Taboo*. There is always an originary crime lurking at the heart of desire.

In a final twist to the story of *Hamlet* at the beginning of psychoanalysis, Carl Jung, in a letter from January 6, 1913—where he splits irrevocably with Freud—writes:

I accede to your wish that we abandon our personal relations, for I never thrust my friendship on anyone. You yourself are the best judge of what this moment means to you. "The rest is silence."

This letter effects the separation between psychoanalysis and what would come to be known as analytical psychology. Freud, in a letter to Sándor Ferenczi in 1925, another in a long line of sons ordained and then discarded, writes about Jung:

The last issue of the *Journal of Nervous and Mental Disease*, August, has an interesting review of a lecture that Jung gave in London in May. Very pretty to see how, in the twelve years since the separation, he also hasn't taken one step further; he is just as benumbed as Adler. Just as clear what a mean fellow he has remained, for he doesn't shy away from the same distortions of analysis that we so frequently trace back to lack of knowledge in others. The remainder—to vary Hamlet's last words: the rest is phrases.

Always identified with Hamlet, Freud's cutting reply is not far from that between Hamlet and the fool Polonius: "What do you read, my lord?" "Words, words, words." Or perhaps better: "My honorable lord, I will most humbly take my leave of you," "You cannot, sir, take from me anything that I will more willingly part withal—except my life—except my life—except my life." Polonius will be slain, the guts dragged under the staircase and used as fodder for jokes. Just because we happen upon a story like that of Oedipus or Hamlet, even love them as much as Freud seems to, elevating their structure into a universal theory, doesn't mean we know how to end the cycle of violence. The birth of psychoanalysis is also a tale of a pile of corpses.

One more story: the savage fight between French Lacanian psychoanalysis and American ego psychology is born out of the soil of Lacan's psychoanalysis with Rudolph Lowenstein. Lacan is reported to have disparaged his analysis on a number of occasions as some sort of process of normalization by a man who furthermore wasn't smart enough to analyze him in the first place. While this is no doubt true—there are few with the genius of Lacan, and Lowenstein is not one of them—what is even more troubling is the fact that Lacan was forced to continue this analysis as the condition of his membership in the Société Psychanalytique de Paris by Princess Marie Bonaparte, who everyone knew was his analyst's lover. This is the very same rich and powerful princess patient of Freud who saved the Fliess letters from the fire, along with infamously engaging in multiple surgeries on her clitoris to cure an apparently incurable frigidity.

Of course Lacan did not continue his analysis once he attained membership in the psychoanalytic society, a fact that greatly angered Lowenstein. Blackmail, it must be said, has no place in psychoanalysis, and Lowenstein, for his part, should have known better. Lacan eventually ruptures his relations with the SPP and is ultimately "excommunicated," as he liked to call it, by the International Psychoanalytical Association in 1963. The icing on the cake, as usual, is found in a letter, and, as usual, *Hamlet* is used to sling insults across the incestuous familial field. Lowenstein, advocating that Lacan's analysands be denied admittance to the Paris society unless they undergo a new analysis, writes:

As regards Lacan's ideas, my view is that he shows penetrating imagination in pursuit of the signifier but has no interest in the signified. With this defect, no scientific discourse, aspiring to be a branch of knowledge, can claim to be complete. And so when I read his work, I can't help thinking "words, words, words." And yet I love and admire Mallarmé.

Brutal. But it says more about Lowenstein than it does about Lacan. Lowenstein, most Hamlet-like, has his eyes on what he calls a defect in the other, one that he sees as tarnishing his ambitious dream of psycho-analysis as a complete science, psychoanalysis with its own branch on the sacred tree of knowledge. The spying of a defect, as we saw with Schmitt, Benjamin, and Hegel, always says more about the voyeur than the observed.

Lacan would go on to found his own school on the basis of this "defect," the signifier, and there is noth-ing sacred or complete for Lacan because of it, least of all psychoanalysis itself. Furthermore, there is noth-ing more detrimental to what Lacan would call "full speech" than the neurotic fantasy of absolute knowl-edge, of being without defect or lack. Yes, we hear Lacan say, Shakespeare! Mallarmé! Such is the world of the word and the world of the word is the life of the world.

Get Thee to a Nunnery

Is THERE ONLY a tale of interminable parricide and infanticide at the origin of psychoanalysis? What about love? Is there not also a story of incestuous passion and unrequited love? In 1912, as the second in a series of essays called *Contributions to the Psychology of Love*, Freud wrote a remarkable paper called "On the Universal Tendency to Debasement in the Sphere of Love." What he tries to articulate in this work is the phenomenon of an internal obstacle, a Hamletized inhibition, that interferes with all conscious intention, which he universalizes under the name "psychical impotence." At its most extreme we are talking about literal sexual impotence, but Freud generalizes from this into a wider set of cultural phenomena. The reason for this obstacle, Freud suggests, is an incestuous fixation that has not been surmounted, and what he shows is that the attempt to surmount this tie emerges as a degradation of the object of love.

What occurs in debasement is a splitting of the object, whereby love is reserved for the overvalued incestuous object and its representatives, while sexuality and sensuality are freely expressed only with an object that is despised. It is with this "not" incestuous representative that devotion to one's own pleasures can be freely experienced, especially without the feeling of being judged or bound. The opposition between the sacred and the profane is an expression of this split, as is the opposition between the virgin and the whore or the good wife and the bad mistress. It must be said that this description is mainly a description of male sexuality in Freud. While Freud sympathizes at one point with the effects on a woman when her partner approaches her without his "full potency," feminine sexuality remained something of a mystery. He stated to Princess Bonaparte, "The great question that has never been answered and which I have not yet been able to answer, despite my thirty years of research into the feminine soul, is 'What does a woman want?' "[13]

For Freud, idealization of the object of love turns us against our own sensuality, yielding a kind of static neurotic nostalgia. "I did love you once," Hamlet confesses to Ophelia in their first onstage encounter, before adding, "I loved you not." From that point on, until he learns of her muddy death, Hamlet never ceases to debase and degrade Ophelia. Freud puts the matter in a nicely Shakespearean oxymoron, "Where he loves he does not desire, and where he desires he cannot love." A certain amount of this splitting between love and desire accompanies all adventures of eros in civilization, hence the adjective "universal" (or, more accurately, "most general" [Allgemeinste]) in Freud's title. Again, the claim is that it is quite impossible to adjust the force of the sexual instinct to the demands of civilization, and a woman's claim to the love and desire of men is thwarted by psychical or physical impotence.

What becomes useless in the sexual instinct then can only appear in the form of dissatisfaction and impotence rather than merely expressing the exigency or necessity of life and love. If eros and civilization do not fit together, then the cost of culture is the price of sexual renunciation, which is perhaps only marginally and harrowingly ennobled with the vague concept of "sublimation." Sublimation, for Freud, requires us to sacrifice the ultimate aim of the drive, namely, satisfaction, through deferment. Only through this sacrifice will we transform libido into an object of cultural veneration, a higher cultural achievement than mere sexual satisfaction. He says, pessimistically, that it is not an option open to everyone. For the rest, debasement beckons, the defense against which is only malaise or massive inhibition.

Freud next takes up the question of love in his 1914 essay "On Narcissism: An Introduction," where he distinguishes a narcissistic desire to be loved from another kind of love, one that is perhaps closer to the conjoining of love and desire. In the former, love is used in order to fill out our own ego through the love object. This narcissistic love is a love of the other as (1) what one is, (2) what one was, (3) what one would like to be, and, (4) someone other than who this loved one is, someone who is already a part of oneself. This love gives a feeling of heightened self-regard, as if we were loved by our own ideal. Our ideal returns back to us in the act of loving in the image of a chameleon's tongue. By contrast, and we will return to this later, the love that exceeds narcissism does not raise self-regard. It leads, rather, to a form of humility and an expenditure of desire. Freud writes:

> The effect of the dependence upon the loved object
> is to lower that feeling: a person in love is humble.

A person who loves, has, so to speak, forfeited a part of his narcissism.[14]

Perhaps this forfeit, Freud goes on to wonder, is the cost at the heart of sublimation. If so, it might be a price worth paying.

Hamlet's Mourning and Melancholia

FREUD'S 1917 PAPER "Mourning and Melancholia" is the kernel of crucial innovations in psychoanalysis, especially those of Melanie Klein, and it is the most important work of Freud's for understanding Lacan's reading of *Hamlet*. If there is a hidden psychoanalytic rival in Lacan's interpretation of the play, a kind of Laertes-like double whose characterization of the lost and loved object he is struggling against, then it is Klein.

In what Freud calls "normal mourning," something absolutely extraordinary takes place. In subjective rather than objective time, individuals who have suffered some loss are allowed to engage in a process of psychical working through. Mourning demands a period of time that is absolutely individual and that we, as a culture—at our best—grant to a person. In a civilization defined by an endless, exhausting, and atomizing experience of labor in which each person has a price in the form of a wage, where our time is never our own, mourning offers a unique experience where we work on our own time, where we take the time we need. We might even say that a condition sine qua non for something resembling a decent culture consists in allowing subjects to take the time they need to mourn. Insofar as that time is not granted, then we might well declare that society is rotten. Of course, this is the rottenness of Denmark in *Hamlet*. The first time we encounter

Hamlet before he learns of the apparition of the ghost, he is addressed by Claudius and Gertrude in exactly the same terms: "How is it that the clouds still hang on you?" says the former; "Good Hamlet, cast thy nighted color off," adds the latter. Hamlet is denied the *time* to mourn.

During the time of "normal mourning" Freud says that the person must go through every memory, every fantasy, every trace connected to the object, and make a judgment: this is my representation—my love, my wishes, my anger, my grief—and in reality this object is gone. Mourning weaves a kind of symbolic tapestry that indicates that the object is lost; it evokes the object *as* lost but also as having been desired. The mourning subject must mourn until finished, shuffling through the one thousand traces connected to the beloved. And there is an end—a decisive one, even—where something seems to lift, the work comes to a close, the "depressed" state falls away, along with the heightened investment in the lost and loved other, leaving desire open.

Melancholia, on the other hand, cannot begin this work. The work of mourning is somehow paralyzed. Freud conjectures that what we see in melancholia is that while one might know that something was lost—a beloved person, a relationship—one does not know what they have lost in them. The object-loss is withdrawn from consciousness. Since Hamlet is denied the time to mourn, to find what he wanted in what has vanished, his grief flips over into melancholia. The demand from his "parents" that he should throw off his inky mourning cloak is met with an unremitting series of puns and pranks that circle round a truth that already escapes expression, "I have that within which passeth show;/These but the trappings and the suits of woe." The problem is that Hamlet cannot say what "passeth show." Being and seeming are sundered. "I know not 'seems'" Hamlet says, but that knowledge that truly is cannot be spoken. Hamlet simply doesn't know what he loves or has lost.

While the lack of interest, the sense of sadness, are present in mourning, what is added to this in melancholia is a disturbance in the sense of self-regard, a strange kind of shamelessness and exhibitionism, where the person abases and degrades himself in front of everyone. "They make the greatest nuisance of themselves,"[15] Freud says. Moreover, while one is confronted with the feeling that everything the melancholic says is true, one is left asking: *And so what?* The psychoanalyst might well conjecture "everything you say is true, but what do you want in it?" In fact, it is precisely at this moment that Freud turns once again to Hamlet. He writes:

It would be equally fruitless from a scientific point of view to contradict a patient who brings these accusations against his ego. He must surely be right in some way and be describing something that is as it seems to him to be. Indeed, we must at once confirm some of his statements without reservation. He really is lacking in interest and as incapable of love and achievement as he says. But that, as we know, is secondary; it is the effect of the internal work which is consuming his ego; work which is unknown to us but which is comparable to the work of mourning. He also seems to us justified in certain other self-accusations; it is merely that he has a keener eye for the truth than other people who are not melancholic. When in his heightened self-criticism he describes himself as petty, egoistic, dishonest, lacking in independence, one whose sole aim has been to hide the weakness of his own nature, it may be, so far as we know, that he has come very pretty near to understanding himself; we only wonder why a man has to be ill before he can be accessible to a truth of this kind. For there can be no doubt that if anyone holds and expresses to others an opinion of himself such as this (an opinion that Hamlet held both of himself and of everyone else ["Use every man after his desert, and who should 'scape whipping"]), he is ill, whether he is speaking the truth or whether he is being more or less unfair to himself. Nor is it difficult to see that there is no correspondence, so far as we can judge, between the degree of self-abasement and its real justification. . . . Finally, it must strike us that after all the melancholic does not behave in quite the same way as a person who is crushed by remorse and self-reproach in a normal fashion. Feelings of shame in front of other people, which would more than anything characterize this latter condition, are lacking in the melancholic, or at least they are not prominent in him. One might emphasize the presence in him of an almost opposite trait of insistent communicativeness which finds satisfaction in self-exposure.[16]

Speaking the truth is not necessarily a sign of mental health for Freud, and perhaps illness and truth telling are more closely allied than we might want to believe. The analyst confirms the truth only in order to finally get beyond it: Yes, yes, you are a wretched failure. Hamlet's suicidal nihilistic apprehension of the meaninglessness of life and everyone's irreparable faults, while true, is nonetheless the linchpin of his melancholia, whose thirst for debasement and self-exposure fuel a noisy and annoying chatter. The problem is a problem of desire, which for Freud must be hardy precisely in the face of truth. Desire opens the way to a tact with truth whose basis is a capacity for shame and true remorse that the melancholic precisely lacks.

For Freud, it is impossible that a simply true state of things—a loss, a revelation—can cause such extreme internal disorder. There must be a structural prerequisite. What he concludes is that love that is too narcissistic has difficulty confronting the object as lost. Instead, the ego and the object collapse, the shadow of the lost object falling on the ego. The object fills the ego with its loss, acting like a gangrenous sore. Object-loss withdraws into the self to avoid, as Freud put it, the extinction of love, and the ego becomes a gaping wound. The person identifies with the lost object and is literally crushed by it. Think of the double meaning of the word *crush,* as in "I have a crush on her," and you'll have some sense of the interplay between loving and melancholia.

This process wreaks internal havoc, even Freud points out, on a biological level. The melancholic typically experiences the inability to draw in energy, like that necessary to allow sleep to happen—life becomes a flat insomniac night. While also, crucially, lacking the ability to direct energy outward—namely, to desire. "How weary, stale, flat and unprofitable / Seem to me all the uses of this world!" Hamlet says. "Man delights not me—nor woman neither." Existence for the melancholic is neither life nor death; it is a ghostly life, a perpetually haunting and haunted liminal space. Mania shows us an energetic flip-flop in a veritable explosion of libido. Mania gives us the twisted surface of melancholia's Möbius strip where depression and enthusiasm join at a hinge that forms at the loved other. One can move between melancholically having no object of desire to everything being a potential object of wild manic humor and sexual excitement; from impossibility to infinite possibility, infinite jest.

Freud also says that a kind of mirror relation between self and other begins to dominate the picture. Reproaches against the self are often reproaches against the lost beloved, and reproaches against one's loved ones are secretly held self-incriminations. This ping-pong blame game increasingly spins out of control. It is here that self-objectification and self-punishment enter the scene as the superego sings its executioner's song. At its most extreme point, Freud says, this punishment is on the path to suicide—literally following the lost object into death. Suicide is always homicide for Freud. One does not kill oneself. One kills the hated other that one has become, and the only means of separation from this object seems to be through literal death.

Why does this happen? Freud speculates that if the attachment to the lost object is fundamentally narcissistic this leaves one vulnerable to melancholia. That is, the loss cannot be "worked through" as a loss. The loss cannot be situated. One might say that the beloved cannot be seen in his or her difference in order to begin the work on what was loved and what was lost. Much like the argument of "On the Universal Tendency to Debasement in the Sphere of Love," Freud feels that in order to deal with loss, the cleavage in the ego must resort to ritualized debasement: in the case of love, debasement of the other; in the case of melancholia, debasement of the self. In this weird and indeed twisted way, love escapes extinction. But the cost is always the disappearance of desire, its fading away. So when Hamlet says to Ophelia "Get thee to a nunnery," this is his way of melancholically and incestuously loving her. Hamlet cannot pay the price required to love—the sacrifice of instinct for the sake of civilization—so his love appears in this mutilated and indeed mutilating form. Such is Hamlet's version of hell.

A Happiness That Often Madness Hits On

THE DRAMA OF Hamlet is that of someone having to force his way out of the failure of the Oedipus complex, which Lacan likens to a failure to mourn. The path to love is neither given nor obvious, having to rest on a desire that is forever bound to the unconscious. The defense against desire, against the life of desire, is nothing short of the work of the death drive—intolerant as it is of anything that raises the level of tension, good or bad. This zero state is similar to what is required in the exigencies of narcissism. For Lacan, this vulnerability to narcissism plays an important role in the failure to resolve our Oedipal complex. Freud stumbled upon this unique human failure:

> Freud replies, as always, without the slightest precaution—he bowls us over, and thank God he did it till the day he died, for otherwise he never could have finished what he still had to lay out in his field of work—Freud replies that it's [the aftermath of the Oedipus compex] a narcissistic demand made by the subject.[17]

Hamlet—melancholic, inhibited, and unable to love—shows us the crossroads between life and death, between narcissism and desire. The demand for un-adulterated life, for the absence of defect, the doing away with loss in the guise of a plea for satisfaction and happiness arises like a "cursèd spite" that Hamlet cannot set right.

Spite hovers somewhere between a subjective meaning, having or doing something out of spite, and the objective injustice of the world order:

> We seem to have lost the sense of this reference to the world order. "O cursèd spite" is what Hamlet feels spiteful toward and also the way that the time is unjust to him. Perhaps you recognize here in passing, transcended by Shakespeare's vocabulary, the delusion of the *schöne Seele* [beautiful soul],[18] from which we have not escaped, far from it, all our efforts notwithstanding. . . . This justifies and deepens our understanding of Hamlet as possibly illustrating a decadent form of the Oedipal situation.[19]

What is decadent is the narcissistic-melancholic aftermath of Oedipus in *Hamlet.* Hamlet, trapped in spite against spite, is caught in an interminable battle where a personal flair for feeling wronged, a sense of inhibition whenever desire makes its appearance, keep him bound to a demand that no longer recognizes what is simply the injustice of the world, the historical moment in which he was born. Hamlet cannot go, headfirst, to meet his destiny, his time.

In *Oedipus the King,* the father's murder is atoned for by Oedipus's castration, a self-blinding self-punishment whose effect is a renewal of the law or one's relation to it. Once the polluting tragic hero has been excised and exiled, the city is cleansed. In *Hamlet,* however, the possibility for this kind of atonement and renewal seems foreclosed. The father is dead, but the crime cannot be paid for; castration cannot be assumed. The demand, or "dread command," of the dead father remains in force, whose consequence is only further loss fueling the continued repression of desire, ad infinitum. A tragic character of loss attends the life of desire in *Hamlet.* If he succeeded, it would be through a kind of willing sacrifice, a price paid for the possibility of sublimation through acceptance of an inevitable loss.

Castration, then, is not a bad thing; it is a heroic achievement in the manner of Oedipus. Only in crossing through what Lacan baptizes "the castration complex"—the humanization of sexuality irrevocably tied to the work of mourning and separation—can we recover our desire. We lack the object of our desire, which acts like a tear in the fabric of our being. Armed only with a swarm of representations—"words, words, words"—we knit a veil to cover this hole.

In *Civilization and Its Discontents,* Freud writes that it is not the hubris of Oedipal desire that is the problem; it is the hubris of happiness. There is no happy, definitive resolution of one's Oedipal trials. Happiness is one more guise of an indiscriminate superego command: Be satisfied! Happiness is a stasis, a powerful calculus that renders desire simply the service of goods. This childish vision takes the form of civilization's dream of progress in the image of man as a prosthetic God. And man, Freud declares, is not happy in this godlike state. The danger of desire is always lurking below the surface, in every tragic encounter at the crossroads.

For Lacan, tragic experience gives us what is sublime about sublimation. We force our desires into a world that is fundamentally opposed to them. Our desires are our ruin, using the Greek word *ate,* which also means "bewilderment," "infatuation," and "rashness." Against all odds, we carve a space for desire. "Everyone," Freud says, "must find out in what particular fashion he can be saved." What Lacan adds to this thought in *The Ethics of Psychoanalysis,* particularly in his reading of *Antigone,* is that one must never give way on one's desire. And, it must be said, Lacan was known for his rashness, his fierce determination, and his unwillingness to yield, even to stoplights, which he was said to run through mercilessly in his car on Parisian streets. Legend has it that when driven, if his chauffeur refused to run a red light, Lacan would get out of the car and walk through it. This characteristic comes to define his psychoanalytic technique: the fifty-minute clock did not tell him when to stop a session; he did it when he pleased.

For Lacan, the sublimation of desire is the most radical achievement of the human subject where the object is elevated and transformed through desire. One can see in this an act that runs counter to the trend of imaginary degradation subtended by Freud. Mourning is the pivot between the selfish sequestering of narcissism and the integrity of desire. As Freud indicates, however briefly, *Hamlet* can be read as containing this unfolding story, the tragedy and sublimity of desire.

At Every Moment Absolutely Stupefied—Lacan Bites the Carpet

THE QUESTION OF DEATH and mourning runs from one end of *Hamlet* to the other. No one in this play really speaks about anything else. The encounter with the ghost is nothing other than the encounter with death itself, which causes a profound estrangement in Hamlet. Gertrude, the unmobled queen, mourns her husband too quickly; Hamlet is accused by his father's murderer of mourning too long; Ophelia, whose father is buried in stealth after being murdered by Hamlet, descends into a psychosis; and Laertes, like Hamlet, loses both his father and Ophelia—both men competing over their grief in a life-and-death struggle that takes place in Ophelia's very grave.

Lacan's reading of *Hamlet* stretches over two months of seminars. Each session functions as a successive pass over the entire play—repeated and repeating elaborations of a developing structure that keeps looping back around in order to gain fresh momentum. When we first began reading this seminar, we did so with no particular interest. In a second pass, we stopped short at Lacan's exclamation in his second session. It is a moment that seems to be a surprise, even to him; and we, looking through Lacan's spectacles, too were surprised. He says:

> For those who read the text, it is something that knocks you over backwards, makes you bite the car-

pet and roll on the ground, it is something unimagi-
nable. There is not a verse of Hamlet, nor one of
his replies, which does not have in English a percussive power, a violence of language which makes of it
something which one is at every moment absolutely
stupefied. You could believe that it was written yes-
terday, that one could not write things like that three
centuries ago.[20]

What is it that knocks Lacan over backward? What
has him biting the carpet and rolling around on the
ground? What in Hamlet is so violent and unimagina-
ble? What can we identify with so strongly even though
it is centuries old? We'd be hard-pressed not to recognize this as a moment of Lacan's desire that we encoun-
tered in such a way that it evoked our own. The force
of this quotation sets the tone for Lacan's entire reading
of *Hamlet.* Whatever this percussive power, this stu-
pefaction, Lacan goes on to say, the play unfurls like
this—as if everyone has their back to a wall of truth
that they cannot recognize and that is hemming in on
them from all sides. It is as if we are caught at a certain threshold where there is no relaxation. The world
becomes a living reproach by which the characters,
and Hamlet best, are ensnared. Hamlet's words seem
to try to shatter this intolerable limit—words that
become a cruelty he unleashes in all directions, first and
foremost at himself. The violence of Hamlet is the violence of failed mourning. This erupts as a melancholic
nihilism, an insistent repetitive harping on the word
nothing.

Lacan conjectures that an intrinsic relation between
time and mourning is staged in the very form of the
play. Hamlet lives at an hour that is never his own and
nothing is more out of joint in this play than time:

When he [i.e., Hamlet] stays on, it is the hour of his parents. When he suspends his crime, it is the hour of the others. When he leaves for England, it is the hour of his Stepfather. It's the hour of Rosencrantz and Guildenstern when he sends them on ahead to death—with a casualness that amazed Freud—by means of a bit of hocus-pocus that he brings off not half badly. And it is the hour of Ophelia, the hour of her suicide, when the tragedy will run its course, in a moment when Hamlet has just realized that it's not hard to kill a man, the time to say "One" . . . he won't know what hit him. . . . He receives word of an event that in no way seems to promise an opportunity to kill Claudius. . . . all in all, it is still at the hour of the Other, and what's more, for the sake of the Other's wager, wearing the king's colors, for his stepfather's sake, that Hamlet enters into this supposedly friendly combat. . . . He rushes into the trap laid by the Other.[21]

Hamlet, paralyzed, proceeding through hesitation and procrastination, only acts in a sudden burst of haste with utter impulsivity. It is as if time is never his own. He arrives too early or too late. The play itself seems to veer around disjointed moments: its long drawn-out beginning, only for Hamlet to be gone for what seems like months, with a final, crazed sequence of events where all parties meet their end.

Lacan declares that you only act when you do not know—that you've killed your father and are sleeping with your mother. When you do know, the consequence of that knowledge is morbid inhibition:

The one who knows is in such a dangerous position as such, so marked out for failure and sacrifice, that he has to take the path, as Pascal says somewhere, of being mad along with the others.[22]

In other words, the only way of dealing with an excess of knowledge is by pretending to be a fool—indeed, of course, this is the entire strategy of the fool in *King Lear*. The truth that Hamlet is exposed to is a hopeless truth, a truth without redemption. If it doesn't make one mad to begin with, like Ophelia, then one has to play a game of madness. For Lacan, Hamlet must assume the coordinates of his life despite life's corruption, and when one assumes desire, it can only happen in an almost purified form—a pure desire for what isn't rather than what is. We act not because of some rational a priori ground but rather in the face of a lack of it—namely the lack that is the ghost. *Hamlet* is this tragedy of desire:

> Insofar as man is not simply possessed, invested by it, but that he has to . . . find this desire. Has to find it at all costs, and in great suffering, to the point of not being able to find it except at the limit.[23]

This limit is that of the self—one's narcissistic framework—that must be traversed. Mourning, as we said, is the pivot between narcissism and desire. The narcissistic capture that Hamlet embodies—this locked, internal tension of inhibition, the pride in the sense of injury—shows us the necessity of desire, its point of relief. Death is always the horizon of this self-shattering, and loss is always in the background of any work with desire. Hamlet can only find his desire when he is literally marked by death, already dead, as it were—"I am dead," he says to Horatio, not "I am dying."

Death desires us, and to desire is to face up to death.

In one of the most severe Lacanian interpretations of *Hamlet,* Stuart Schneiderman radicalizes the point at which death and desire are intertwined. Hamlet can only kill Claudius when the act of revenge is revenge for his own death. It is not, for Schneiderman, a facing up to death; it is just one more act of refusal on Hamlet's part. Hamlet fails to escape the traps of narcissism, and in this view he is a coward through and through. Schneiderman's is perhaps the most damning of interpretations:

> When he does it, it is too late, his act no longer means anything, it no longer has its ethical edge. The murder of Claudius is an afterthought, which Hamlet, as Lacan said, can only accomplish when he is dying, when he will not have to bear responsibility for his act. Even more important is the fact that Hamlet acts when he learns that the wretched Claudius is responsible for Hamlet's impending death. Hamlet can avenge himself because he is an egoist to the end, especially at the end. With his dying breath he asks Horatio to tell *his* story. . . . Hamlet is clearly a failure—he cannot act on his desire, he can only perform the act he is obliged to perform when it is no longer his desire—and his success is to convince the audience that it is no failure at all, that we can still love him.[24]

We can see why the figure of Antigone—in love with death, as Creon says—becomes the quintessential hero of desire for Lacan. She is beyond fear and self-pity.

That Is Laertes, This Is Hamlet

WE KNOW OF the profound effects of the ghost not from Hamlet but from Ophelia, to whom he "raised a sigh so piteous and profound as it did seem to shatter all his bulk and end his being." Hamlet, shaken by the appearance of the ghost, attempts to recover from what Lacan calls a fundamental alienation and estrangement. The ghost shatters Hamlet. For Lacan, the play can be read as a restaging of the "unfolding dialectics of desire" after Hamlet is 'loosed out of hell.' " Lacan is putting to the test his stage theory of desire. The play is like an attempt at reknotting anew the strings of one's being that have come undone, which is essentially the task of psychoanalysis itself. Desire must be resurrected in Hamlet.

Classically, melancholia is situated under the category called the narcissistic neuroses, meaning it is grouped together with the psychoses, the obvious culprit what we now commonly call schizophrenia. Indeed, melancholia can lead to psychosis, and its structure is more problematically narcissistic than the neuroses proper—hysteria, anxiety hysteria, the obsessional, and phobia. Already, you can see Lacan's shift away from Freud's definition of Hamlet as a mere hysteric. He is following the structure that Freud outlines in "Mourning and Melancholia."

What is lost must be resituated as such—Hamlet

knows *whom* he has lost, but not *what* he has lost in them. Desire is something between you and your ideal. Desire carves a space between oneself and an image of wholeness that can hold a subject captive. Desire exists in a transitional space on the limit of life and death. The object of love is wrapped in this liminality, symbolically given life by a desire that begins to represent it. When this representational world falls apart, it perhaps first collapses into an impossible ideal, a source of neurotic nostalgia or a degraded and debased object of hate, disgust, and rivalry. In this collapse it is as if we cannot bear the distance, the gap, between what is and what we wish was.

Encountering the one thousand guises of loss in the work of mourning stays the slide toward zero. The lost other is literally composed of desire. And this loving desire, infinite though it may be, brings us face to face with loss. As a certain controversial French philosopher once put it, between the two of us, we know that one of us will die first, "one of us two will see himself no longer seeing the other."[25] The inflection is always on the impact the possibility of death makes on one's self-image. The essence of mourning is that we will one day have to say good-bye, adieu, *à Dieu,* to let our beloved go to God.

So what Shakespeare's play plays out is the movement between this absolute estrangement of Hamlet by the ghost, the retreat from desire and fall into narcissism, and finally the attempted reconstitution of the object of desire and its reintegration. It is this mourning drama of desire—between like others, like siblings and rivals, who provide a mirror image of ourselves, and a much bigger other, a terrifyingly strange unknown,

"the undiscovered country"—that Lacan begins to outline through his reading of *Hamlet*.

In Lacan's interpretation, the play's ending—the
rapier fight with Laertes—is motivated when Hamlet,
watching Laertes mourn at Ophelia's funeral, leaps at
him in her grave. He lets out an otherworldly cry of grief
in an act of odd self-nomination, "This is I, Hamlet
the Dane." This is the only moment of self-nomination
in the play, and, of course, in doing so he bears the
name of the father. The first-person level of identification only seems to become possible by way of a passage through the grammatical form of the impersonal
third person in a scene of interpersonal struggle. More
precisely, Laertes embodies Hamlet's self-image in the
form of an ideal and thus functions as a kind of double.
It is only through his double that Hamlet is able to find
something of his desire in relation to the dead Ophelia,
and it is precisely this desire that gives him back his
name, Hamlet.

This happens in a moment of seeing himself, outside of himself, positioned in relation to the lost
Ophelia, situated through intense conflict with a rival.
Laertes's grief bears such emphasis for Hamlet that it
"conjures the wand'ring stars and makes them stand
like wonder-wounded hearers." Hamlet seems, for
a second, not lost. Wonder-wounded, his ear opens.
He hears something that brings him to the point of
announcing his very self-presence. He says to Laertes:

> I loved Ophelia. Forty thousand brothers
> Could not, with all their quantity of love,
> Make up my sum. (*To Laertes*) What wilt thou do
> for her?

Like the play within the play, we access something as intimate as desire in a moment outside of ourselves—in a flash of identification with the other's desire. As Hamlet says later of Laertes, "to know a man well were to know himself." This is also the very structure of theater, both the theatricality of drama and the mise-en-scène of psychoanalysis.

But the travesty is that it does not hold. Hamlet cannot find a way to support his desire through this other, his double. Shortly after this proclamation, his love veers off as he turns to Laertes—"What wilt thou do for her?" The competition grows fierce, wild, and, one might even say, quite mad:

> 'Swounds, show me what thou'lt do.
> Woo't weep? Woo't fight? Woo't fast? Woo't tear
> thyself?
> Woo't drink up eisel, eat a crocodile?
> I'll do't. Dost thou come here to whine?
> To outface me with leaping in her grave?
> Be buried quick with her, and so will I.
> And if thou prate of mountains, let them throw
> Millions of acres on us, till our ground,
> Singeing his pate against the burning zone,
> Make Ossa like a wart! Nay, an thou'lt mouth,
> I'll rant as well as thou.

He'll eat a crocodile for her, but it is not his love Ophelia whom he is to be buried with but Laertes in his competition with him—an uncanny foreshadowing of the ending. All Hamlet does do, more than Laertes, is rant and mouth off. Perhaps that is to be expected.

We are always outfaced by a double. Our image in the mirror gets the best of us. If we cannot support desire's outward movement, desire degrades internally into narcissistic woundedness, a sense of being subjectively outstripped and objectified. Take the conclusion to this scene. In a moment of what we infer to be total misrecognition, Hamlet says to Laertes: "Hear you, sir. What is the reason that you use me thus? I loved you ever." Laertes is using Hamlet in crying for his dead sister? Who is using whom? And why is being used even the stakes of their relationship? Laertes's father has been killed by Hamlet himself, something you would imagine he could at least identify with, and yet Laertes is nothing but a source of contention. And while he has always remarked on his love for Ophelia in the past tense, which has finally caught up with her corpse, with Laertes his love is eternal, perhaps only because it is to himself in the mirror that this love is directed.

So if Laertes is Hamlet's double, then it is no surprise that the play ends with their double murder. We have two groups, one a reduplication of the other: Polonius, Laertes, Ophelia; and Claudius, Hamlet, and Gertrude. By the end of the play Laertes is uncannily in the same position as Hamlet: he has a father murdered, Ophelia lost, the support of the rabble for the throne; he acts as an organ for Claudius's scheming, and he desperately seeks revenge:

> And so have I a noble father lost.
> A sister driven into desp'rate terms,
> Whose worth, if praises may go back again,
> Stood challenger on mount of all the age
> For her perfection. But my revenge will come.

Happily, we are spared the apparition of the ghost of Polonius. But it is almost as if Hamlet must construct this double in order to kill him, a foil in his revenge against the king. Only through Laertes's mourning and his rivalrous identification with him can he find his own mourning. Only through Laertes's condemnation of the king—"The king. The king's to blame"—does he finally take revenge. Hamlet is always trying to catch up to this other, to an image of himself. Like two mirrors placed in front of each other, we can see the trap of reflective reflexivity, the point of infinite regress where you receive back your own image or message in inverted form. As Lacan will remind us, the French expression for "thou art" *tu es,* "you are," is phonetically indistinguishable from the verb "to kill," *tuer.*

The Image of My Cause I See—
Hamlet and the Mirror

THE MIRROR IMAGE never fails to captivate and alien-
ate. Self and self-image, ego and ego ideal, oscillate
between idealization and aggressivity, erotomanic love
and murderous rage. Perhaps this explains Hamlet's
almost incomprehensible vacillation when speaking of
Laertes. After their fight at Ophelia's funeral, Hamlet
calls Laertes "a soul of great article" and extols his virtues to the messenger till he literally exhausts speech.
One cannot help but think he "doth protest too much,"
but then again, this is a matter of love in the mirror, a
perverse peculiarity contained in the very ode:

> Sir, his definement suffers no perdition in you,
> though I know to divide him inventorially would
> dozy th'arithmetic of memory, and yet but yaw nei-
> ther, in respect of his quick sail. But, in the verity of
> extolment, I take him to be a soul of great article,
> and his infusion of such dearth and rareness as, to
> make true diction of him, his semblable is his mir-
> ror, and who else would trace him, his umbrage,
> nothing more.

One cannot divide an ideal, he is the image only of
himself, complete—"his semblable is his mirror." To
copy him is an ambition that would prove itself nothing but a bad dream, self evaporating into shadow.
Lacan summarizes it:

In brief, the reference to the image of the other, as being that which cannot but completely absorb the one who contemplates it, is here, in connection with the merits of Laertes, certainly presented inflated in a very over-elaborate, conceited way, is something which has all its value at that moment. All the more since, as you are going to see, it is with this attitude that Hamlet is going to approach Laertes before the duel. It is on this footing that he approaches him and it only becomes more significant that it is at this paroxysm of imaginary absorption . . . a mirror reaction, that there is also situated by the playwright the manifest point of aggressivity.[26]

This is the one moment Hamlet ceases to speak about himself—in order "to make true diction" of Laertes. And if this quiets him, it is because he is on the path toward manifesting his aggression. It will happen on the basis of Laertes's call, not his own. He has to hear his own message from his mirror and then attack it, attempting to dominate and reincorporate the piece of himself glimpsed through the image.

Thus the function of the mirror is one of misrecognition. How else could we explain why Hamlet ends up fighting Laertes *for* Claudius when he is to be avenging Claudius himself? How, in light of this, could Harold Bloom have written that Hamlet comes home to Denmark in act 5 a changed man? The Hegelian dialectic shows that "the person you most admire is the one that you fight. The one who is the ego-ideal, is also, according to the Hegelian formula of the impossibility of co-existences, the one you must kill."[27] Or as Lacan puts it brutally in his eponymous essay "The Mirror Stage as Formative of the I Function":

> Existentialism can be judged on the basis of the
> justifications it provides for the subjective impasses
> that do, indeed, result therefrom: a freedom that is
> never so authentically affirmed as when it is within
> the walls of a prison; a demand for commitment
> that expresses the inability of pure consciousness to
> overcome any situation; a voyeuristic-sadistic ideal-
> ization of the sexual relationships; a personality that
> achieves self-realization only in suicide.[28]

We couldn't have better characterized the action of the
play.

The mirror stage has its origins in Lacan's doctoral
dissertation on the case of Aimée, the story of a woman
whose psychosis culminated in stabbing the celebrated
Parisian actress Huguette Duflos. Lacan treated her
during her hospitalization at Saint-Anne in Paris and
was fascinated by the fact that this brutal act seemed
to stabilize her illness. He developed a theory of what
he called "self-punishment paranoia" where the other is
delusionally punished as a mirror of the self, as a semblable. Passionately loving the other as our ideal is fundamentally unstable—a mirror, lest we forget, freezes
an image in a symmetry that also reverses it. Like children who cry when they see others fall, the boundary
between self and other still retains this fluidity in the
special trap of a reversible mirror. Following this logic,
children who feel guilty often provoke punishment,
a punishment that quiets and calms them, redefining
the boundary of self. The questions, Am I bad? Am I
guilty? find an answer.

Freud remarked that the experience of the double
is uncanny, on the border of life and death, as if what
is most intimate and hidden suddenly appears outside
in an apparition, looking at you. Narcissistic psycho-

sis for Freud is a final radical break with the world, as if the love that one uses to see something outside is a cord that can snap completely, recoiling inward. It is experienced as a silent apocalypse, whose philosophical correspondent is nihilism. The double functions as a tie for a desire that is in the process of fragmenting and withdrawing. Even in its extreme form—in paranoiac delusions—this image of the other that we create is potentially curative, albeit in a strange and tragic way. Delusion acts like a cradle for this withdrawal of love, giving the subject a place in the world again even in the fanatical form of having a hated omnipotent persecutory other. At least, we might say, there is someone rather than no one, and moreover this someone is parasitically attached to us. Their gaze is supported by this call to vigilance. As Freud will eventually point out in his 1921 work, *Group Psychology and the Analysis of the Ego,* this is close to how a heterogeneous group consolidates into a mass—namely, through an external enemy. In this basic Schmittian paradigm, the dictatorial decision follows shortly thereafter.

Both melancholia and paranoia involve delusions of self-punishment, indefatigable ambivalence, the distortions of self-perception, and a rupture within desire. As the most extreme form of mental illness, psychosis reveals the pathological, but still universal, underpinnings of the superego, the problems inherent in any ideals or idealism, and the violent fiction that is our ego. Taken together, melancholia and paranoia give new meaning to the superego in its original German form, *das Über-Ich,* the over-I. The superego, seat of the death drive, springs from our infantile attachments to parental figures of authority, those who, for a time, stood over us, kept watch on us, and dispensed punishment. Sickness is the malady of narcissism in its most extreme form as the aural obscenity of the superego (think of the characteristic hearing of voices, often persecutory, in schizophrenia). The point of excess in our parents' punishments, no less ideals and love, returns in this disembodied form—the dread command of the ghost. A young toddler left in a room to play can often be heard repeating the range of parental tonal improprieties using the mere word "no." It is this intergenerational transmission of thanatos that twists eros into internal debasement.

Desire goes from being precarious to deadly. Lacan calls this *passage à l'acte,* what we might call "acting out," a moment not unlike Hamlet jumping into Ophelia's grave after Laertes. As Hamlet says about it to Horatio after the fact:

> But I am very sorry, good Horatio,
> That to Laertes I forgot myself,
> For by the image of my cause I see
> The portraiture of his. I'll court his favors.
> But sure the bravery of his grief did put me
> Into a tow'ring passion.

The unfolding of desire in the mirror is a fragile moment that can lead straight "Into a tow'ring passion." There will never be enough room for both figures in the mirror. The double strips us of the autonomy and independence originally sought. Hamlet forgets himself, seeing himself externally, Laertes the image of his cause. The double is the double edge of the defining outline that we seek in supposedly feeling "ourselves." It is the most extreme moment of the failure and misrecognition inherent in narcissism. We are always haunted by the instability of this line between self and other, threatened by what lies beyond ourselves, uncanny and monstrous. As Hamlet warns Laertes, "I have something in me dangerous / Which let thy wiseness fear."

The man in the mirror is the first blossoming of desire in Hamlet in the form of his double. It is with Laertes on the one hand, and Horatio on the other, that Hamlet speaks with an admiration whose potential for serving as the basis of his own desire can be patently felt, as if you only had to push him across this threshold, beyond the mirror. Hamlet's desire manifests between these two others, the ideal and the rival, acting out his revenge, then meeting his end.

Ophelia, or the Sexual Life of Plants

OPHELIA IS THE embodiment of fierce femininity, the rock of love and the bedrock of castration—and, as such, she is the true casualty of the tragedy. It is from her that the real threat emanates. If Hamlet's identification with Laertes serves as an opening onto desire, pretty Ophelia is in the reverse position. She acts, in her life, as a pure obstacle. Not only Hamlet, in fact, but most of the other characters in the play—Polonius, Laertes, and also the king and queen—dismiss Ophelia as someone who possesses her own desire. She is always taken as something to be used, as *bait*. No one ever asks her what it is that *she* wants. In her madness we see her desire explode onto the stage, immersed in a voracious sexuality invariably denied to her. From this, she slips into the river and dies. The scene is described through her clothing: "mermaid-like" and incapable of her own distress her dress becomes heavy with "drink." In this play, we are never very far from the dimension of orality, which we are beginning to suspect is why it has Lacan biting the carpet. Nowhere is the play more orally violent than in the encounter between Hamlet and his women. And nowhere is the play more sexual than with Ophelia's mad singsong language of plants and flowers, a language of desire that becomes the scene of her death on the riverbank, merging with her image on the surface of the water.

Ophelia, reaching for long purples, which "liberal shepherds give a grosser name, / But our cold maids do dead men's fingers call them," surrounded by nature, its "pendant boughs" her "weedy trophies," tumbles down into the "weeping brook" and drowns. With an eerie equivalence between death, the phallus, and the potent, flushing sexual vitality of flora, Ophelia dies on a bed of flowers like Hamlet's father in the dumb show. While the flowers she bestows upon herself seem to bear on the concealment of sexuality—long purples associated with the male member and daisies with dissembling—the others are given theirs in kind. Laertes is given rosemary and pansies for remembrance and thoughts, respectively. Gertrude is given fennel and columbines, associated with unfaithfulness. Claudius is also given daisies as well as rue, or "herb of grace o'Sundays," for repentance and sabbatical virtue. She says that he must wear them "with a difference"—in line with Claudius's lesser place in the family lineage. Ophelia would have given him violets, denoting faithfulness, but "they withered all" when her "father died." She speaks the truth through flora, the pure pain of desire with no mediation: the flower's organs are all on the outside.

We are reminded of a dream Freud tells of in *The Interpretation of Dreams* from one of his female patients called "in the language of flowers." She sees herself climbing down over some palisades holding a blossoming branch in her hand that reminds her of a spray of white lilies held by the angel in a depiction of the Annunciation. But she had changed the white flowers to red in the dream, and by the time she reached the end of her climb, their color had faded—what Freud sees as an unmistakable allusion to virginity, menstruation, impregnation, and menopause. Further, there is reference to Dumas's novella *La Dame aux camélias,* which is about a courtesan who usually wears a white camellia except during her menstruation, when she wears a red one. The thoughts in the dream circle around flowers and the problems of sexuality, sin, guilt, and the decline of one's fecundity, beauty, and feminine value. Plants and flowers provide an unusually clear reference to the pains and pangs of desire, filtered through religion, morality, and the special mortality rate of a woman's fertility. Freud, in fact, calls the book on dreams his botanical monograph, his houseplant, where a wish springs from the dream's navel like a mushroom from its mycelium. Desire literally flowers. Freud's dream book is always botanical.

Of course, Georges Bataille will point out that this dream is also a nightmare.[29] The attraction and repugnance of sexuality shines in Bataille's essay "The Language of Flowers." Pushing Freud's dream logic, Bataille writes that flowers, far from representing the ideals of love and beauty, should be seen in their most base materiality—they are nothing but the genitals of a plant. We give flowers not because we love but because we want to fuck:

> Even the most beautiful flowers are spoiled in their centers by hairy sexual organs. Thus the interior of a rose does not at all correspond to its exterior beauty; if one tears off all of the corolla's petals, all that remains is a rather sordid tuft. . . . Risen from the stench of the manure pile—even though it seemed for a moment to have escaped in a flight of angelic and lyrical purity—the flower seems to relapse abruptly into its original squalor: the most ideal is rapidly reduced to a wisp of aerial manure. For

flowers do not age honestly like leaves, which lose nothing of their beauty after they have died; flowers wither like old and overly made-up dowagers, and they die ridiculously on stems that seemed to carry them to the clouds. It is impossible to exaggerate the tragicomic oppositions indicated in the course of this death-drama, endlessly played out between earth and sky, and it is evident that one can only paraphrase this laughable duel by introducing, not as a sentence, but more precisely as an ink stain, this nauseating banality: *love smells like death.*[30]

Life and death, vitality and rot, love and carnal sexuality, cannot be dissociated in the visage of a flower. Ophelia is the very tragicomedy of love, whose main commerce has always been this "death-drama" exchange of flowers as genitals. Their perfume is a momentary veneer, the budding excess that will soon reverse into rot and manure. In Hamlet's words, "'tis an unweeded garden / that grows to seed: things rank and gross in nature / possess it merely." Savagely, and most Shakespeare-like, Bataille points out, that this is the fate of young girls who bloom and wither almost simultaneously, their flushed cheeks already the image of the paint put on by an old dowager in imitation of her younger self.

These kinds of insinuations around Ophelia's "maidenhood"—her status as both a sexual object and a girl supposed to be purified of sexuality—are her undoing. "O, woe is me, T'have seen what I have seen, see what I see!" What is she if she is defined by the price of an impossible feminine sexuality? Nothing? "[A] fair thought to lie between maids' legs"? As she puts it in her crazed eloquence, "They say the owl was a baker's daughter. Lord, we know what we are, but know not what we may be." The option "to be" is not for her, only maybe "not to be," which is why she knows only too well the value of desire. While desire gives the status of being to men who imagine themselves its arbiter—Hamlet knows he will be king—Ophelia is closer to the truth of desire: what you win you instantly lose. Ophelia is closer to her actual being: she is run through by loss. She sings this cutting contradiction to Gertrude in songs replete with phallic imagery:

> How should I your true love know
>> From another one?
> By his cockle hat and staff,
>> And his sandal shoon.

Namely, I know my love by his cock, and his cock, and his cock. But to know of this love is to lose herself:

> To-morrow is Saint Valentine's day,
>> All in the morning betime,
> And I a maid at your window,
>> To be your Valentine.
> Then up he rose, and donned his clothes
>> And dupped the chamber door,
> Let in the maid, that out a maid
>> Never departed more.

She is nothing when she departs; her virginity lost. She continues:

> By Gis and by Saint Charity,
>> Alack, and fie for shame!
> Young men will do't, if they come to't.
>> By Cock, they are to blame.

> Quoth she, "before you tumbled me,
>> You promised me to wed."

He answers:
"So would I ha'done, by yonder sun,
      An thou hadst not come to my bed."

Ophelia is a tumbled daughter. She has been possessed and discarded in an identification—no less
objectification—where she merges with the dead.
Ophelia returns to incestuous sheets, reunited with her
father, both slain by her capricious lover. In fact, the
love odes above are punctuated by songs of her father's
death, "he is dead a gone, lady. He is dead and gone."
And "larded with sweet flowers which bewept to the
grave did not go with true-love showers." Ophelia bids
farewell to Gertrude and Claudius, "I hope all will
be well. We must be patient, but I cannot choose but
weep, to think they should lay him i'the cold ground."
We give flowers to lady lovers and the dead. Ophelia
and Hamlet Senior die on a bed of flowers.

Ophelia acts as a barometer throughout the play
for Hamlet's position with respect to his desire. Her
desire provokes his. As we said, it is through her that
we first learn of Hamlet's wild estrangement, seemingly
half mad, after the encounter with the ghost. After
which time, Hamlet can do nothing but violently reject
Ophelia—he no longer has any desire for her. It is only
with Ophelia's death, in the scene with Laertes that
we've just described, that Hamlet is in any possession of
it again. The play thus seems to turn around Ophelia,
who is its empty center, its *O,* its ground zero. Unlike
Hamlet's feigned antics, Ophelia's psychosis is real;
where Hamlet grieves, cannot act but simply acts out,
Ophelia's grief produces her acts of madness, and she
follows her desire all the way to her death. Ophelia is
the Antigone within *Hamlet.* Arguably, Ophelia is not
just the main casualty in *Hamlet* but its true tragic hero.

The Moneying of Love

WE COULD SEE Ophelia as the only figure in the play with ethical integrity. She stays true to her desire, even in madness. Ophelia is a lesson on the dangers of desire, and it is precisely for this desire that she is impugned, reduced to an object, told that her love is a commodity that she must let her father broker lest her value be downgraded.

When Polonius asks his daughter what is going on between her and Hamlet, Ophelia replies, "He hath, my lord, of late made many tenders / Of his affection to me." Polonius instantly monetizes the amorous language of *tendresse:*

> . . . Think yourself a baby
> That you have ta'en these tenders for true pay,
> Which are not sterling. Tender yourself more
> dearly.

The language of love becomes the language of money, and marriage a commercial transaction. Ophelia needs to raise her price and not be duped by shiny counterfeit coin. Hamlet realizes this when Polonius says, "I have a daughter—have while she is mine," and proceeds to call him a "fishmonger," a pimp. For Polonius, who is invested in his daughter like a life-insurance package, Hamlet's love is false coin for which she must not trade her "maiden presence"—that is, her virginity. This is not because Hamlet does not love her but because he will not marry someone of her status, the daughter of a senior courtier, being himself next in the line to the throne.

For Polonius, Hamlet's tenders have no legality, and she must invest more wisely:

> Do not believe his vows, for they are brokers,
> Not of that dye which their investments show,
> But mere implorators of unholy suits,
> Breathing like sanctified and pious bawds.

Hamlet's vows of love should be treated like those of a sanctimonious brothel keeper. This is also the advice that Laertes gives Ophelia earlier in the scene, insisting that she should not open her "chaste treasure" to his "unmastered importunity." She must fear Hamlet, not love him. Ophelia gets the message, comparing herself to a chastity belt and declaring her brother the keeper of the keys, "'Tis in my memory locked, / And you yourself shall keep the key of it."

All over Shakespeare one can find this collapsing of love into the language of money, a moneying of eros. From the first lines of *The Merchant of Venice*, it is clear that Antonio's entire being is defined in monetary terms. When Shylock says that Antonio is a good man, and Bassanio asks if he has heard otherwise, Shylock replies:

> Ho no, no, no, no: my meaning in saying he is a good man, is to have you understand me that he is sufficient.

But this is simply the echo of Antonio's own elision, when speaking to Bassanio, of his "purse" and "person":

> My purse, my person, my extremest means
> Lie all unlock'd to your occasions.

Personality is pursonality. But Antonio's purse is empty, for his argosies with portly sail are also far-flung, all abroad in Tripoli, Mexico, the Indies, England, and the whole imagined geography of the commercial orb of which the *urb* of Venice is both the mirror and the marketplace. The *urb* of Venice is the orb of the emergent world market and a prospect of what Elizabethan London might turn into in the ensuing centuries. So Bassanio uses Antonio's name, his good name, to gain credit from the usurer, Shylock. In the scene with his mother, Hamlet speaks of "the fatness of these pursy times," where "Virtue itself must pardon beg." In a counterfeit world of forgery, only the ghost is described as "Truepenny."

Consider Shakespeare's sonnets, from whose outset we are treated to a litany of economic terms and conditions: increase, contract, abundance, waste, "niggarding," or miserliness. Sonnet 4 is typical in this respect:

> Unthrifty loveliness, why dost thou spend
> Upon thyself thy beauty's legacy?
> Nature's bequest gives nothing, but doth lend,
> And being frank, she lends to those are free:
> Then, beauteous niggard, why dost thou abuse
> The bounteous largesse given thee to give?
> Profitless usurer, why dost thou use
> So great a sum of sums, yet canst not live?

If you don't reproduce, you can leave no "acceptable audit." The entire argument of the sonnets is that the poet's unnamed and unknown addressee must invest his beauty in a wife in order to have a child and thus to see long-term profit on his investment. Otherwise:

> Thy unused beauty must be tombed with thee,
> Which, used, lives th'executor to be.

As in *The Merchant of Venice,* the interplay of "use," "abuse," and "usurer" cannot escape the reader's attention. Shakespeare returns to this grouping in sonnet 6, arguing again for natural reproduction:

> That use is not forbidden usury,
> Which happies those that pay the willing loan.

A "willing loan" is the opposite of one that is "self-willed": the latter option will make you "death's conquest and make worms thine heir."

This is the image presented to Morocco, Portia's first suitor in the casket lottery by which her body and estate will be given away in *The Merchant of Venice.* Saturday-night game shows and reality television have never gone this far, not even in Japan. Morocco's casket contains a death's-head and a poem about tombs and worms, contents that condemn him to a life of self-willing (onanism) or homosexuality—both "unnatural," forbidden forms of expenditure, abuses rather than good usages of seminal (and here we use the word in all its senses) credit. The pun on "willing" and "willed" also recalls Portia's complaint that "the will of a living daughter" is "curb'd by the will of a dead father." In sonnet 135 this word "will" appears thirteen times:

> Whoever hath her wish, thou hast thy Will,
> And Will to boot, and Will in overplus;

> More than enough am I, that vex thee still,
> To thy sweet will making addition thus . . .

And so on. Will is desire, testament, Shakespeare's proper name and sexual organ, both male and female: the poet at one point saucily requests to "hide my will in thine," "whose will is large and spacious." This hermaphroditic ambiguity also appears in sonnet 20, whose effeminate male addressee, "the master mistress of my passion," was "for a woman . . . first created":

> Till nature as she wrought thee fell a-doting,
> And by addition thee of me defeated,
> By adding one thing to my purpose nothing . . .

That is, "she pricked thee out for women's pleasure." Will, prick, is surplus: adding one to nothing. Portia uses exactly the same trope in *The Merchant of Venice* when proposing her and Nerissa's transvestitism: men "will think we are accomplished with what we lack."[31]

Polonius is Ophelia's guardian pimp, protecting his investment and his bloodline through securing her virginity. This transaction in Shakespeare is always tragic. Ophelia herself is explicitly tied to three women from antiquity, Hecuba, Niobe, and Jepthah's nameless daughter. These women, while being images of fecundity and objects of barter, reverse into the image of the abject and bereft, shown lacking all that they supposedly possessed, left weeping infinite tears. Hecuba is sold into slavery, unable to produce any more sons after the war that took her children and her husband's life. Niobe is punished for pride in her fecundity, all her children slaughtered, and weeps even after having been turned to stone. And Jepthah's daughter must be sacrificed by her father in a vow he made to God and is given two months to mourn for the life she will never have, the children she will never bear, the love that will meet no fruition. Ophelia, as we know, goes mad, which if we translate into the moneying of love means she is worthless. Her only option in this language of exchange is suicide. She declares herself bankrupt and expires.

Thou Common Whore and Visible God

Karl Marx—good, Shakespeare-reading German that he was—liked to quote from *Timon of Athens,* where money is described as both "Thou common whore of mankind" and:

> Thou *visible god,*
> That solder'st *close impossibilities,*
> And mak'st them kiss.

Money is the visible God and common whore of mankind. That is, there is nothing that money cannot solder together, no two commodities for which money will not be the pimp that permits the exchange. It is the imperial empyrean that makes possible the circulation of commodities. In a mercantile society, everything is for sale, and everyone is a prostitute insofar as value is ultimately determinable in monetary terms. Money is the fishmonger between need and object. It makes available all objects and objectifies all beings.

Perhaps this explains why the most circulated insult in *Hamlet,* which the Danish prince ceaselessly hurls at himself, is to call someone a whore, a drab, a wanton, a strumpet, a bawd, a harlot, to name a few. In *The Ethics of Psychoanalysis,* Lacan sets up a basic antinomy between an object degraded to mere exchange and one sublimely elevated to the level of the Thing, *das Ding.*

The latter is a kind of purified object whose singular value is created by one's loving desire. Antigone animates what Lacan calls the still-living corpse of her brother. In the vein of Kant, who describes purposeless beauty as a flower, it is only in what cannot be turned into an object of utilitarian purpose that one can find the radiant splendor of beauty. Or as Hamlet puts it in his unflagging language of negation:

> The power of beauty will sooner transform honesty from what it is to a bawd than the force of honesty can translate beauty into its likeness. This was sometime a paradox, but now the time gives it proof.

For Hamlet, in his despair, Ophelia has become one more potential seed of corruption. She shows, in her innocence, the worm that gnaws at the heart of a bud. He cannot love her any longer, and in any case, as he says, she should not have believed him. If one cannot desire, life is condemned. Hamlet plunges into a narcissistic withdrawal. Much as Freud describes, Ophelia collapses into the debased female object that Hamlet violently repudiates: "get thee to a nunnery"; "wouldst thou be a breeder of sinners"; "I say we will have no mo marriage." Nowhere has an object of desire been dissolved with such cruelty than in Hamlet's rejection of Ophelia. The scene with Hamlet is harrowing, vicious, ruthless:

> HAMLET: If thou dost marry, I'll give thee this plague for thy dowry: be thou as chaste as ice, as pure as snow, thou shalt not escape calumny. Get thee to a nunnery, go: farewell. Or, if thou wilt needs marry, marry a fool, for wise men know well enough what monsters you make of them. To a nunnery, go, and quickly too. Farewell.

OPHELIA: O heavenly powers, restore him!
HAMLET: I have heard of your paintings too, well
enough. God has given you one face, and you make
yourselves another. You jig, you amble, and you
lisp, and nickname God's creatures, and make your
wantonness your ignorance. Go to, I'll no more
on't, it hath made me mad. I say, we will have no
more marriage. Those that married already—all
But one—shall live. The rest shall keep as they are.
To a nunnery, go.

Ophelia, handed over to Hamlet as bait by her
father and the king and queen, is destroyed by this
speech of callous debasement. She is accorded no room
for her desire. Her dowry is exchanged for this plague.
Claudius and Polonius themselves do not show even
the remotest concern for her following this scene; her
father merely lets her know that she need not report
back; they witnessed it all. The next time we see her,
she will be mad.

The structure of this act of debasement is important when considering the traps and pitfalls inherent in
this treacherous crossing between the shores of narcissism and those of desire. The debasement of the object
comes in the place of desire. It is as if one can only
desire in this disfigured form. Lacan says of it with
regard to Ophelia:

She is no longer the reference-point for a life that
Hamlet condemns in its essence. In short, what is
taking place here is the destruction and loss of the
object. For the subject the object appears, if I may
put it this way, on the outside. The subject is no
longer the object: he rejects it with all the force of
his being and will not find it again until he sacrifices
himself.[32]

Hamlet cannot sacrifice anything. He cannot tolerate loss. Ophelia becomes the pure virginal offering. Ophelia's fecundity is an offense, her life and life-giving body, whose swell he'd rather imagine as dried up and rotting. These complaints are, one must remember, reproaches he has held against himself—ho, hum—trying to force this ideal outside in the form of this degraded loved one. You are the plague! He even tells Ophelia that were she to remain chaste as ice and die a virgin, she would not escape unmarred. And so she doesn't. But neither will Hamlet.

For Lacan, captivated as he is with "hysterics," Ophelia is a powerful representation of desire in its negative form as abject dejection. Sometimes desire is evoked best in its movement of disappearance, in the case of Ophelia as she is in the process of being discarded, wasted, lost:

> Ophelia is [. . .] one of the most fascinating creations which has been proposed to human imagination. Something which we can call the drama of the feminine object, the drama of desire, of the world which makes its appearance at the dawn of civilization in the form of Helen . . . incarnated in the drama and misfortune of Ophelia.[33]

One can imagine why she has inspired so many paintings, her repose in the river always depicted as a state of grace that is only hers when she has finally become nothing. Like the object in mourning, the lost object par excellence, Ophelia appears in her very impossibility—the lost object at the dawn of civilization. Her death acts, even if only for a moment, like a second encounter with death that allows something of Hamlet's own mourning to finally take place. He animates Ophelia's corpse. But as we saw in the scene with Laertes, Hamlet turns away from her toward rivalry and revenge. She is dropped, even in death. Only Gertrude eulogistically raises Ophelia up again. And it isn't clear why Gertrude should be the one to narrate poor Ophelia's fate. But it is the one time we hear Gertrude speak, as a woman with compassion for another woman, and perhaps most important, with a palpable sense of grief. Ophelia's melodious death, sirenlike, awakens in the "beast" Gertrude a voice of mourning.

Gertrude, a Gaping Cunt

So let us consider the other woman in *Hamlet*. Ophelia is coupled with Gertrude, Hamlet's mother, the only mother in the play. What happened to Ophelia's mother? Gertrude and Ophelia are the two feminine figures circulating in the play, and in their interplay, the displacement of the rage from Hamlet's mother to his would-be wife, who will never be a mother herself, we find the Oedipal key to the question of his desire. Lacan famously said (with some impetuousness that may offend) that Gertrude is a gaping cunt, *un con béant*. Mourning means nothing to her—when one goes, another comes. Hamlet's mother's love appears in the image of a revolving door.

In this configuration, the object is always degraded to the level of base utility, or what Lacan calls an object of *jouissance*. The latter literally means "orgasm" or "enjoyment," but the range of connotations in French include death, *la petite mort*, pain mixed with pleasure, and an experience at the limit. For Lacan, symptoms are an expression of desire caught in the grip of *jouissance*, caught in a repeating loop, that is both the repetition compulsion of a kind of narcissistic-masturbatory sexuality of energic discharge and the compulsion to repeat our own and our parents' traumas. Psychoanalysis helps a patient refuse this *jouissance* in the direction of desire. It is this life of desire that we see Hamlet try and fail to find in relation to Ophelia and his mother. His encounter with them is like an encounter with a culture of death—they are beasts that eat men. Hamlet can only find separation in an empty call to the order of modesty and decency. "A little propriety, please; there is all the same a difference between this God and that filth," as Lacan allegorizes it playing out in Hamlet's mind in the "counterfeit presentment of two brothers," Hamlet's two fathers.

But it is not the discrepancy between this Hyperion that was his father and the mildewed ear that is his stepfather that troubles Hamlet, one that cannot, in any case, be as stark as all that. Hamlet is searching for desire, in the name of king and country, of virtue and beauty; we might say, in the name-of-the-father. This attempt repeatedly reaches a sheer pitch of idealization from which it sinks back down, into filth, into rags, into shreds and patches. The splitting of the object, Lacan says, has its corollary in the fading of the desire of the subject. These two moments—one on the side of the subject and one on the side of the object—are dialectically intertwined.

Desire cannot be approached when its interior void feels so menacing. An oral, greedy wanton desirousness in them threatens Hamlet, of whom his mother is the consummate sinner. The problem for Hamlet is not *his* unconscious desire for his mother. It is his *mother's* desire that is a problem. What does Gertrude want? It is the enigma of Gertrude's desire that drives Hamlet into a wild rage. For Lacan, and this is certainly a twist in Freud's reading, with the death of his father Hamlet is thrown back upon the desire of his mother in a kind of melancholic identification. He cannot separate from her. He is fixated within her desire. Crushed by his mother's desire at every step, Hamlet slides into an obsessive contemplation of her. In his first soliloquy:

> Must I remember? Why, she would hang on him
> As if increase of appetite had grown
> By what it fed on—and yet within a month—
> Let me not think on't: frailty thy name is woman!
> A little month, or ere those shoes were old
> With which she followed my poor father's body
> Like Niobe, all tears—why she, even she—
> O God, a beast that wants discourse of reason
> Would have mourned longer—married with my
> uncle,
> My father's brother, but no more like my father
> Than I to Hercules. Within a month,
> Ere yet the salt of most unrighteous tears
> Had left the flushing in her gallèd eyes,
> She married. O, most wicked speed, to post
> With such dexterity to incestuous sheet!

If his mother pleads with him in the opening scene, "let not thy mother lose her prayers, Hamlet," his answer "I shall in all my best obey you, madam" is the one oath that Hamlet sustains. "Nothing in him can oppose in short a sort of fundamental availability . . . hiring himself literally to another and again for nothing."[34] Ultimately he never confronts his mother with the truth that he has learned from the ghost of his father. She learns it only as she dies. And maybe not even then, for all that Gertrude knows is that she has been poisoned by Claudius. After Hamlet sees Gertrude die, he learns of his own poisoning, and only in the short interval between her death and his own does he finally avenge his father's murder. He proceeds, to the very end of the play, in lockstep with his mother's desire.

For Lacan, to understand this configuration requires an elaboration of Freud's original interpretation of the play. What Freud thought so correct and obvious in Hamlet proves more complicated. Why, for example, should his Oedipal desire for his mother not lead him to kill Claudius swiftly?

> We see him when all is said and done with two ten-dencies; the over-riding tendency which is doubly commanded him by the authority of his father and the love which he bears him; and the second of wanting to defend his mother, and of wanting to keep her for himself, which ought to make him go in the same direction and kill Claudius. Therefore two positive things, this is a curious thing, will give a zero result.[35]

In other words, why do two ones make zero? Why does love for his father and possessiveness of his mother not send him toward the act of revenge?

The problem is Hamlet's relation to desire. His desire is preoccupied with his mother's desire. More generally, the psychoanalysts will conjecture that Hamlet is preoccupied with the "phallus" that he imagines her as having—either in the form of Claudius or in the very flush of her sexual appetite. The phallus is the imaginary object that Hamlet wants to be for his mother so that she does not want anything more. You cannot be the thing that you imagine completes the other, the psychoanalyst warns. When all is said and done, this is simply an incestuous-melancholic fantasy: Hamlet caught in the position of wanting to be the man that he is to avenge, wanting his mother not to want, or rather not to want anything besides himself. So he always turns back to her, in reproach after reproach, scene after scene.

Hamlet cannot reach a level of sublime freedom, a failure of desire that he assails in everyone but always Gertrude first. Hamlet will be compelled to either repeat or work through his relation to his mother's desire. As he himself asks, "Is there no sequel at the heels of this mother's admiration?" His symbiotic tie with Gertrude is played out in front of us as Hamlet, time and again, slides into Gertrude's place in his very speech. He literally speaks from the place of his mother, never his own.

Desire must cut through this mirroring melancholic identification. Some act of mourning must cut through this pride of injury in relation to his mother. The function of the father, for Lacan, is this cut—a ghost, a shade, a thing of almost nothing. And the one imperative given to Hamlet by his father's ghost is to let his mother be:

> But howsoever thou pursuest this act,
> Taint not thy mind, nor let thy soul contrive
> Against thy mother aught. Leave her to heaven
> And to those thorns that in her bosom lodge,
> To prick and sting her.

The ghost, Lacan says—and it is an elegant piece of interpretation—is this cut, this piece of the real that cannot be assimilated. The ghost is the point of unbearable loss. It calls on Hamlet. Remember me and leave her to heaven, to the prick and sting of her own conscience. Remember me, and revenge my most foul and unnatural murder.

The ghost of Hamlet's father always appears to intervene in the space of this cut, between Hamlet and his mother—beseeching Hamlet not to, to step back, to purify his desire of this preoccupation, to remember his duty there where he needs to most: precisely, in the face of his mother. The ghost pleads with Hamlet, trying to drive a wedge between his desire and hers, knowing that Hamlet is bereft of his desire, his purpose blunted, "duller" than "the fat weed that roots itself in ease on Lethe wharf." The ghost pleads with him to hear—"List, list, O list"; "lend thy serious hearing"; "so art thou to revenge, when thou shalt hear"; "now, Hamlet, hear." Hamlet, unable to hear the ghost's message, commits the perfect act of parricidal incest. Relinquishing his promise sworn to the ghost, Hamlet bounds toward his mother. The vision is one of the family in ruins, the end of a lineage by the play's conclusion, the father's ghost reappearing in an attempt to restore an order that has already been torn asunder.

Mother, Mother, Mother

AFTER STAGING THE play within the play, Hamlet catches Claudius defenseless in a moment of prayer and *does not kill him*. He has his evidence, his chance, yet he procrastinates. It is "hire and salary," he says, not revenge. Hamlet dreams of a moment of cataclysmic violence, interrupting Claudius in a moment of incestuous passion, in his criminal phallic brilliance, cut off in the blossom of his sin, as was Hamlet's father. An Oedipal fantasy if there ever was one:

> Up, sword, and know thou a more horrid hent.
> When he is drunk asleep, or in his rage,
> Or in th'incestuous pleasure of his bed;
> At gaming, a-swearing, or about some act
> That has no relish of salvation in't;
> Then trip him, that his heels may kick at heaven,
> And this his soul may be as damned and black
> As hell, whereto it goes. My mother stays:
> This physic but prolongs thy sickly days.

Imagining barging in on the primal scene, the incestuous pleasure of Claudius's bed, and sticking it to him gives Hamlet the impetus *not* to act, and instead he goes to his mother. It's not the right time (it's never the right time). The Claudius he wants is not the one who genuflects. If there is something inexplicable about this stepping down, this fantasizing, the inhibition that washes over Hamlet, we will learn of it in this scene with his mother.

Hamlet, before encountering Gertrude, tries to give himself reproof—Do not lose your temper with her, hold firm:

> O heart, lose not thy nature. Let not ever
> The soul of Nero enter this firm bosom.
> Let me be cruel, not unnatural.
> I will speak daggers to her, but use none.
> My tongue and soul in this be hypocrites.
> How in my words somever she be shent,
> To give them seals—never, my soul, consent!

We will bear witness to the failure of this cautionary tale. The scene with his mother is sheer, almost intolerable, excess. The reading of this scene is the heart of Lacan's interpretation of Hamlet:

> And there takes place this long scene which is a kind of high point of theater, this something about which the last time I told you that to read it brings you to the limit of what you can tolerate, where he is going to adjure his mother pathetically to become aware of the point that she is at.[36]

Hamlet cannot steady himself in the face of Gertrude, blurting out almost immediately, "Mother, you have my father much offended." Eros grows violent, and violence grows increasingly erotic as he approaches her, Gertrude immediately crying out "what wilt that do? Thou wilt not murder me? Help, ho!" Taking matters too far, we think the lady doth protest too much. Gertrude's own pornographic sadomasochistic fantasy breaks into the scene. In a concomitant response of rash haste, Hamlet kills Polonius, asking if it is the king—his uncle-father—whom we know he has just left outside. "Thought-sick at the act," indeed. He even confuses his mother with Claudius: "A bloody deed? Almost as bad, good mother, as kill a king, and marry with his brother." Claudius and Gertrude merge in Hamlet's imagination, something we see repeated in his mocking reply to Claudius after he sends him to England:

> HAMLET: For England?
> CLAUDIUS: Ay, Hamlet.
> HAMLET: Good.
> CLAUDIUS: So it is, if thou knew'st our purposes.
> HAMLET: I see a cherub that sees them. But, come, for England! Farwell, dear mother.
> CLAUDIUS: Thy loving father, Hamlet.
> HAMLET: My mother. Father and mother is man and wife. Man and wife is one flesh—and so: my mother. Come, for England!

It is always one flesh for Hamlet. Gertrude, of course, cannot hear anything that Hamlet is raving about, "Ay me what act that roars so loud and thunders in the index." One might give her some lenience and ask, How could she? The guilt of Hamlet's mother, as Schmitt was right to point out, is like a dark spot in the play. After this confusion of tongues, Hamlet begins his appeal to Gertrude—a message also no doubt meant for himself, eerily given in this inverted form:

> The hey-day in the blood is tame, it's humble
> And waits upon the judgement, and what judgment
> Would step from this to this? Sense sure you have,
> Else could you not have motion, but sure that sense
> Is apoplexed, for madness would not err,

Nor sense to ecstasy was ne'er so thrilled
But it reserved some quantity of choice
To serve in such a difference. What devil was't
That thus hath cozened you at hoodman-blind?

Is this not a description of Hamlet? The one who errs
such that there is nothing left of choice in serving a
dispute. The devil that "cozened you," the same doubt
that Hamlet holds toward the ghost in his soliloquy on
the deception of theater. Is this not the very selfsame
devil?

Confronting his doubts about the ghost through
reproofs against his mother, Hamlet comes upon the
devil in her that is *not* his father. His discourse reaches
a pitch of fury, now centered on a description of his
mother's body,

Eyes without feeling, feeling without sight,
Ears without hands or eyes, smelling sans all,
Or but a sickly part of one true sense,
Could not so mope.
O shame, where is thy blush? Rebellious hell,
If thou canst mutine in a matron's bones,
To flaming youth let virtue be as wax
And melt in her own fire. Proclaim no shame
When the compulsive ardor gives the charge,
Since frost itself as actively doth burn
And reason panders will.

This call to temperance bleeds into an almost fanati-
cally excited description of Gertrude's desire. Cloaked
in a call to shame, his words mount in tension, the high
point of this percussive penetrating power, where he
finally reaches her in bed: "Nay but to live in the rank
sweat of an enseamèd bed, stewed in corruption." From
this semen-soakèd bed, Hamlet airs his grievance—this

thief! Claudius is "a cutpurse of the empire and the rule, that from a shelf the precious diadem stole and put it in his pocket." The language of love, as with Ophelia, is reduced to a language of money. The moneying of eros as Hamlet's inheritance takes the pain of loss and betrayal and transforms it into a paranoid fantasy about some "thing" stolen by the devil pimp that he finds lurking in the shadows of his mother's ardor. Melancholia takes what is lost and gives to it a juridical flair of criminality, theft, what is unjustly taken, and then seeks compensation if not retribution. The moneying of love is also love's legalism.

Claudius is a king "of shreds and patches." Lacan says of this phrase:

> Another trace is that the rejection, deprecation, contempt that he casts on Claudius has every appearance of *dénégation*.[37] The torrent of insults that he unleashes on Claudius—in the presence of his mother, namely—culminates in the phrase "a king of shreds and patches." We surely cannot fail to relate this to the fact that, in the tragedy of Hamlet, unlike that of Oedipus, after the murder of the father, the phallus is still there. It's there indeed, and it is precisely Claudius who is called upon to embody it. Claudius' real phallus is always somewhere in the picture. What does Hamlet have to reproach his mother for, after all, if not for having filled herself with it?[38]

It is no doubt this confusion around what Lacan calls the phallus—adhering in Hamlet's contempt mixed with admiration for Claudius—that leads Hamlet to know neither what has been stolen nor where his grievance lies. Whose crown? His, or his father's? And is this crown, in any case, the throne, his father's life, or his mother's body? Hamlet's grievance escapes, or exceeds from another angle, the truth of his father's dread command. Like a pure demand, we hear his voice like the shrill cry of a baby, asking for everything, anything, from his mother. It is the demand for an object that is not really hers to give, Lacan's very definition of love. It is up to Hamlet to find his loving desire. And Gertrude will not, or rather cannot, hear the truth in what Hamlet is saying.

Step Between Her and Her Fighting Soul

"SPEAK NO MORE," Gertrude cries out five times, writhing beneath Hamlet's insults. At the moment he summons his mother to see her husband as a thieving king of putrid fragmentation, his father's ghost suddenly appears:

> Do not forget. This visitation
> Is but to whet thy almost blunted purpose.
> But, look, amazement on thy mother sits.
> O, step between her and her fighting soul!
> Conceit in weakest bodies strongest works.
> Speak to her, Hamlet.

The ghost asks Hamlet to step between her and her fighting soul. "Speak to her," the ghost implores. To which Hamlet meekly and pathetically asks, "How is it with you, lady?" Lacan says:

> This place where Hamlet is always being asked to enter, to operate, to intervene, is here something which gives us the real situation of the drama. . . . It is signifying to us [psychoanalysts] because this is what is in question for us, what intervening means for us: "Between her and her," that is our work. "Conceit in weakest bodies strongest works," it is to the analyst that this appeal is addressed.[39]

Hamlet, "O wonderful son that can so 'stonish a mother," fails to see Gertrude's amazement. That Gertrude, cleft in twain, could be spoken to. This is the exact moment when one *can* speak. Amazed, astonished, stunned, surprised, she is open, she is able to hear. Speak to her.

The ghost, if we may put it like this, attempts to usher a cut like the interpreting psychoanalyst. It asks Hamlet to step into a space, into the cut of this in-between, into the interval of desire. The analyst interprets "between you and your love." This is what psychoanalysts offer with their words. "Conceit in weakest bodies strongest works": this is what our patients tell us.

Hamlet will only find this space in the form of a literal wound, a mortal and poisoned cut. He cannot hear the message of the ghost any more than he can speak the truth to his mother. As she utters the word "ecstasy," Hamlet careens back into his relentless rant. What follows this scene with the ghost is one more act of stepping down, where we see the disappearance, the dying away, of his appeal:

> Laying down his arms before something which seems ineluctable to him; namely that the mother's desire here takes on again for him the value of something which in no case, and by no method, can be raised up.[40]

And Hamlet sends her back to Claudius, tells her to let him kiss her neck and denounce him as mad. Hamlet cannot speak from the position of "I, Hamlet" about his father but only from his mother's position—what she will be for Claudius, and Claudius for her. It is such a strange moment:

> Not this, by no means, that I bid you do:
> Let the bloat king tempt you again to bed,

Pinch wanton on your cheek, call you his mouse,
And let him, for a pair of reechy kisses,
Or paddling in your neck with his damn'd fingers,
Make you to ravel all this matter out,
That I essentially am not in madness,
But mad in craft.

And so she does. When Claudius asks, "How does Hamlet?" she replies, "As mad as the sea and the wind, when both contend, which is the mightier." In this moment, Hamlet

abandons his mother, he literally allows her to slip, to return as one might say to the abandonment of her desire. And here is how this act finishes, except that meanwhile the unfortunate Polonius had the misfortune to make a movement behind the arras, and Hamlet has run his sword through his body. We come to the fourth act. There is something here that begins very nicely, namely the hunt for the body.[41]

Why the hunt for the body after this scene with his mother? Hamlet is always trying to find something to penetrate the enigma of desire, which he too often mistakes for the phallus, searching for a noble king in the dust. Lacan turns our attention to what Hamlet says in his feigned madness when he stashes the body beneath the stairs: the body is with the king, but the king is not with the body; the king is a thing, a thing of nothing,

I would ask you to simply replace the word King by the word phallus in order to see that it is precisely what is in question, namely that the body is engaged in this affair with the phallus, and how, but on the contrary, the phallus itself is not engaged in anything . . . it always slips between your fingers.[42]

Hamlet chases butterflies; their beating wings singeing Hamlet with an anxiety that sends him bounding down a winding path. The phallus is a ghost, an illusion, nothing but a shade: "For it is as the air invulnerable, and our vain blows malicious mockery." It always escapes. It is nothing—namely, nothing real. The phallus is nothing but a signifier of desire that you mistake for your being. Crossing the castration complex means bearing this news, enduring its cut.

Hamlet wants the phallus, so he cannot pay the pound of flesh in which it has become absorbed—the price for any access to desire. He cannot sacrifice that portion of his narcissism, which, in any case, would require submitting to his destiny in the form of the call of a ghost. Taking on the debt of existence—an existence replete with a father's crimes, a mother's sin, and one's own ambitions—is perpetually refused. This negativity in desire is what Hamlet must assume, but cannot. He always holds on to himself, even if only through constant mad chatter.

By contrast, Oedipus pays for his crimes through his singular act of self-castration. At the end of *Oedipus the King,* it is not the scales that fall from his eyes but his eyes that fall like scales, reduced, as Lacan says, to being castration itself—living blind and in exile. Everything Oedipus thought was substantial is shown to be an illusion: brought to naught. Hamlet, in the slow, zigzag, mad progress of the play, also finally pays, but with his life—letting the action pass through him. He never dirties his hands.

We might ask whether this is paying for anything, since Hamlet lives with none of the consequences of the desire that courses through him, inherited—as desire always is—from his family. The play ends not with his exile but with his country's, his family left in ruins as "th' election lights on Fortinbras." Hamlet's inheritance and the lands from Hamlet's father's war are given to Norway. "Remember me" indeed. The grace of desire and the memory of the mourned are elided. Denmark becomes a Norwegian dominion.

The Oedipus complex, as Freud tirelessly shows, leaves behind its wounds, its scars. When we come to the end of this affair, the loss is always radical. The play, as we said, ends in a pile of corpses. It is not our own death—which we have known, since Epicurus, that no one can experience—but the deaths of others that rend the fabric of our being. From this perspective we can see the most radical position of the subject in the very negativity of this loss. Either the belief in the phallus is retained through the refusal of mourning or it disappears and we gain access to our desire. Take your pick or, perhaps better, take your prick.

Who Calls on Hamlet?

WE SHOULD NOT forget that there is a bad psycho-analyst in *Hamlet:* "I have found the very cause of Hamlet's lunacy." Polonius, who insists, in his foolish etiologic diagnostics, that the cause of Hamlet's mad-ness is the ecstasy of his love for Ophelia, a character-istically self-serving interpretation by a man who talks too much and too much in the language of clichés. Psychoanalysis has suffered since Freud's death, having given way to the banalities of pop psychology and the moralisms of the day, holding to rote notions of causal overdetermination by some supposed historical real-ity, as if we easily understood history, no less "reality." Whose reality? Lacan always asks. And in the case of Hamlet, such a smug Polonius-like psychoanalyst can be found saying, "Hamlet's problem is he cannot love," to which Lacan will also ask, "And you can?"

The Truepenny psychoanalyst in Hamlet is the ghost, who cuts between ourselves and our fighting souls, who recognizes the strength of conceit in the face of the weakness and mortality of our bodies. The ghost's very essence throughout popular myth seems to fol-low from a truth at the heart of psychoanalysis—we are doomed to phantasmic repetition, to haunting and being haunted, in relation to a lack of satisfaction that must be situated as such. The ghost offers us access to our desire and so also our destiny, but it is an offer that is treacherous, if not tragic. "O cursèd spite." And the sole ethical injunction of psychoanalysis is not to give way on that desire that is within you:

> Psychoanalysis alone recognizes the knot of imaginary servitude that love must always untie anew or sever. Psychoanalysis can accompany the patient to the ecstatic limit of the "Thou are that," where the cipher of his mortal destiny is revealed to him, but it is not in our sole power as practitioners to bring him to the point where the true journey begins.[43]

The modesty of analysts is such that they only issue a call. This is what you are! It is not in their power to set any human defect, if there even is such a thing, right. They can only help to bring you toward a gap in yourself, a place of radical loss in the abyss of desire. Give yourself to it.

Part III

Nietzsche Contra Nietzsche

In 1886, a few years before his final, apoplectic collapse from the probable effects of tertiary syphilis, Nietzsche wrote a short preface to his first book from 1872, *The Birth of Tragedy*. It was called "Attempt at Self-Criticism." It is one of the greatest examples of philosophical honesty ever written. In his ferociously analytical, relentlessly incisive, comical, and indeed slightly crazy mature style, Nietzsche tears into his early work like Agaue into her son Pentheus in Euripides's *The Bacchae*. He calls *The Birth of Tragedy* a questionable book, an impossible book:

> I consider it badly written, ponderous, embarrassing, image-mad and image confused, sentimental, in places saccharine to the point of effeminacy, uneven in tempo, without the will to logical cleanliness, very convinced and therefore disdainful of proof, mistrustful even of the *propriety* of proof, a book for initiates.[1]

But that is not the worst of it: for the "initiates" Nietzsche speaks of here are those of Richard Wagner, the dedicatee of *The Birth of Tragedy*, whom Nietzsche fantasizes about receiving his book, "perhaps after an evening walk in the winter snow." In the deeply flawed second half of *The Birth of Tragedy*, Nietzsche asserts that a rebirth of tragedy might be possible through the music of Wagner. But it gets even worse. It is not just the cultish Wagnerism of the young Nietzsche that appalls the writer of the 1886 preface; it is the *Germanism*. Nietzsche confesses that "On the basis of the latest German music, I began to rave about 'the German spirit.'" For the mature Nietzsche, the Germans are "a people who love drink and who honor lack of clarity as a virtue." If Germanity is a kind of damp fog, then the antidote is not a shift to humanity, but to Latinity, which leads Nietzsche in his very last writings into an arguably misplaced adoration and elevation of Bizet's *Carmen.* In *The Case of Wagner,* from 1888, Nietzsche writes that "Wagner's art is sick." Yet, the painful pathos of Nietzsche's late writing is that he knows that Wagner's sickness is also *his* sickness, which requires a profound, cold self-estrangement and sobering up. This is what Nietzsche does in the 1886 preface, where he reads himself with a hammer.

In *Ecce Homo,* written shortly before his final collapse, he returns one last time to *The Birth of Tragedy* and looks to the future. Of course, looking to the future is easier for Nietzsche than for others, as he promised he would be born posthumously. He confesses that, despite the many stupidities of *The Birth of Tragedy,* its Schopenhauerianism, its Wagnerism, its Germanism, all of which sounds "offensively Hegelian,"[2] "a tremendous hope speaks out of this writing." This is the hope for "a Dionysian future of music." He looks a century ahead, when his *attentat,* or "assault" on two millennia of antinature has been successful. We then hear some of Nietzsche's disturbing eugenic discourse on "the higher breeding of humanity" and the fearful and fateful allusions to "the remorseless destruction of all degenerate and parasitic elements." He goes on to add,

"I promise a tragic age: the supreme art in the affirmation of life, tragedy, will be reborn." Nietzsche, then, doesn't lose faith in the possibility of a rebirth of tragedy. His faith is transposed. And how is it transposed? It is *renamed,* to be precise. Nietzsche writes that "a psychologist"—Freud, for example, think of the logic of semantic inversion that will often proceed lexically in a joke or a slip of the tongue—might have heard in Nietzsche's youthful homosocial attachment to Wagner something that had nothing to do with Wagner and everything to do with someone else—namely Nietzsche himself. "In all the psychologically decisive passages" of a text like "Wagner in Bayreuth," Nietzsche insists that he is the only one named, not Wagner. Therefore, and this is amazing, he suggests that "One may ruthlessly insert my name or the word 'Zarathustra' wherever the text gives the word Wagner." When Nietzsche writes "Wagner," he is not referring to another but to himself. More precisely, he is referring to himself as another.

And so we are back to the theme of doubles and doubling. And this is problematic, of course. If the later Nietzsche abandons his adoration of Wagner, and his former love for the master becomes hatred, then, via the logic of the mirror, that hatred becomes self-hatred that flips around into intense self-love. In the "antic disposition" of Nietzsche's late prose, we witness a kind of oscillation between a manic autoeroticism, where the object of love is himself, and the collapse or switching over of that discourse into reflexive self-laceration. Such are perhaps what Nietzsche calls "the neuroses of health," the pendulous oscillation between melancholia and mania.

Like the Danish prince, Nietzsche both turns against his doubles and becomes them: Socrates, Christ,

Saint Paul, Schopenhauer, and Wagner. And also, most Hamlet-like, he turns against himself, particularly his younger self, where the name "Nietzsche" seems to describe the division of the subject, a self inauthentically and utterly divided against itself. A self that is not one but that is at least two and that becomes the supreme ironist of itself, writing an autobiography where he identifies with Christ—*Ecce Homo,* behold the man-God—and that is full of chapters called "Why I Am So Wise," "Why I Am So Clever," and "Why I Am a Destiny." Nietzsche, as he says of his double Socrates, is the ironist of ironists. This is why he is so funny, so brilliant, and so dangerous. The problem with doubles is very simple, as we saw with Laertes and Hamlet: two of you are one too many. If you meet your double, be sure to kill him.[3]

Spectatorial Distance

EXTREME AS THEY are, we are not going to take issue with Nietzsche's criticisms of *The Birth of Tragedy*. Indeed, we are inclined to add a criticism of our own under the heading of what we will call the question of *spectatorial distance*. As is well known, Nietzsche takes a rather dim view of Euripides. Nietzsche's claim is that Euripides puts the spectator on the stage and that he is the tragic poet of what Nietzsche calls *aesthetic Socratism*. There are two spectators in *The Birth of Tragedy:* if the first spectator is Euripides, then the second, whom Nietzsche refers to as "the deity that spoke through"[4] Euripides is neither Apollo nor Dionysos but Socrates. This is what brings Nietzsche to the awful calumny—that he must have known to be fallacious—that Socrates helped Euripides write his plays. The problem with bringing the spectator on the stage is that in so doing Euripides brings the "masses onto the stage"[5] and thus debases the stately elevation of Attic tragedy with the stench of democracy, the pollution of the polloi. The axiom of aesthetic Socratism is that to be beautiful, everything must be intelligible (*verständig*).[6] The fantasy—a word which we do not mean pejoratively, as we don't believe that there is psychical existence without fantasy—that underpins Nietzsche's account of tragedy and that leads him to speculate on its birth is the fantasy of the Dionysian as the location of what he calls, in his Schopenhauerian revelry, the *Ur-Ein,* "the primal one," in other words *being,* the key concept in any metaphysics. This is what he elsewhere calls "the mystery doctrine of tragedy"[7]— namely that the Dionysian is the mysterious primal unity that is prior to nature's dismemberment into individuals, the *principium individuationis* that defines the Apollinian. The vehicle or conduit for access to primal being, to a true metaphysics of nature, is the chorus, the satyric chorus, which Nietzsche describes, in a far-from-neutral image, as the *womb* of tragedy.[8]

The Nietzschean fantasy is a metaphysical return to the womb, or at least a contact with the womb, the mother of being, mother *as* being. Tragedy, then, insofar as it remains close to the womb of its birth, allows for contact with the primal one, a kind of pre-cognitive, affective merging where, through the Apollinian beautiful appearance, illusion, or, better, shine (*die schöne Schein*) of the tragic hero, we gain insight into that which is through the chorus and, more specifically, through the spectacle of music and dance. For Nietzsche, it is the god Dionysos that we hear in the *mousike* of tragedy, which means "words plus music." This fantasy of merging, the dissolution of any spectatorial distance, is what drives Nietzsche's account of the birth of tragedy, and it is what he thinks gets lost at the moment of tragedy's death or, more properly, suicide at the hands of Euripides. Consider the primal horde fantasy that Nietzsche expresses in the opening pages of *The Birth of Tragedy* when he seeks an image to describe the Dionysian:

> Transform Beethoven's "Hymn to Joy" into a painting; let your imagination conceive the multi-

tudes bowing to the dust, awestruck—then you will
approach the Dionysian.[9]

Following Freud's *Group Psychology and the Analysis of
the Ego,* one has to be careful of the crypto-authoritarian
fantasy of merging with the other, the formation of the
mass group around a charismatic leader. If the name of
that leader in antiquity is Dionysos, the primal father
who is murdered in tragedy, then we might ponder
the names of its modern representatives, particularly
given Nietzsche's remarks about the rebirth of tragedy
through German music as a return to itself (*eine Rück-
kehr zu sich selbst*) of German spirit. When Euripides is
alleged to put the spectator onstage, it is the possibility
of this merging through the chorus to establish contact
with the Dionysian that disappears.

For us, however, Euripides does not represent a
falling away from the origin as much as a revealing
of what tragedy has always been about: to return to
the quote from Gorgias with which we began, tragedy is always something spectated; it always involves
a theoretical or cognitive distance. Against the young
Nietzsche's authoritarian fantasy of merging, we want
to emphasize that tragedy is always "theoretical"; it
always involves temporal disjunctions between the past
and the present and the felt disjunction between an old
order of myth or custom and a new regime of individ-
uality and law. Tragedy is not some prephilosophical
expression of a traditional way of life but is the formal articulation of the dissolution of tradition and the
diremption of theory and praxis, an experience of the
essential self-division and decay of ethical life. In tragedy, ancient or modern, the time is always out of joint,
and something is always rotten in the order of the state.

The young Nietzsche, like so many others before and after, exoticizes the prephilosophical Greeks. Against this, we recommend a strategy of *de-exoticization* through nothing more difficult than reading the tragic dramas. To say this is not the same as saying that we are in the same situation as the Greeks. Not at all. It was a long, long time ago and far, far away. But tragedy does not have to wait until Euripides in order to be overcome by rationality. The tragedies of Aeschylus and Sophocles are replete with argumentation, where persuasion (*peitho*) is unleashed by opposed parties to state a disagreement or, in some cases, to try to resolve one. Tragedy is not the belated expression of some prerational ritual. And indeed—as countless anthropologists will attest—there is rationality inherent to ritual itself. What the exquisitely rational dialogues between opposed characters in tragedy show is not the primacy of rationality or the subordination of tragedy to reason but reason's attempt—a failed attempt, moreover—to give voice to what one might call the *uncontainable*.

There is something uncontainable in the experience of tragedy. Nietzsche's name for this uncontainable dimension is the Dionysian. This is not wrong, but there might be other names for this unassimilable power, what the great German poet Hölderlin sees as the monstrous (*das Ungeheuer*), the coupling of the human and the god at the core of the tragic or, for us, the force of *desire*. Where Nietzsche is profoundly right is in his understanding of the effects of Platonic dialogue on the phenomenon of tragedy. As we said in the introduction, the invention that Plato called *philosophia* is the attempt to produce a rival discourse to the *theatrokratia* of Athenian democracy. In *The Republic*, the institution of that rival discourse in the education of the Guardians requires the exclusion of tragedy and the tragic poets. In the concluding book 10 of *The Republic,* this exclusion takes the form of a *metaphysical* critique of imitation (*mimesis*) as thrice removed from the order of truth and a *moral* critique of the excessive affect that is witnessed in tragedy, in particular the affect of lamentation and grief. In this picture, Platonism is the attempt to contain the uncontainable, desirous, and monstrous dimension of tragic experience through a regulation of excessive affect that is always linked to the feminine and to mourning.

By contrast, we might say, Nietzsche reads tragedy in order to *defend a form of philosophy that is excluded by philosophy, what we might call a tragic philosophy,* a philosophy that tries to mark the place of the uncontainable without seeking to contain it. We should recall that, in the discussion of *The Birth of Tragedy* in *Ecce Homo,* Nietzsche describes himself as "the first *tragic philosopher.*" And he goes on, "Before me, this transposition of the Dionysian into a philosophical pathos did not exist: *tragic wisdom* was lacking."[10]

Lethargy and Disgust

In *The Birth of Tragedy* Nietzsche gives a fascinating short interpretation of *Hamlet.* Pulling back from the rather upbeat argument he had been developing about the coupling of the Apollinian and Dionysian that finds expression in Attic tragedy, and whose core is expressed in the satyric chorus, Nietzsche goes on to make the following series of surprising and brilliant remarks, where something like a more independent and mature voice is heard for the first time:

> For the rapture of the Dionysian state with its annihilation of the ordinary bounds and limits of existence contains, while it lasts, a *lethargic* element in which all personal experiences of the past become immersed. This chasm of oblivion separates the worlds of everyday reality and of Dionysian reality. But as soon as this everyday reality re-enters consciousness, it is experienced as such with nausea or disgust [*Ekel*]: an ascetic, will-negating mood is the fruit of these states.
>
> In this sense the Dionysian man resembles Hamlet: both have once looked truly into the essence of things, they have gained knowledge, and it disgusts them to act [*es ekelt sie zu handeln*], for their action could not change anything in the eternal essence [*Wesen*] of things; they feel it to be

ridiculous or humiliating that they should be asked
to set right a world that is out of joint [*die aus den
Fugen ist*]. Knowledge kills action; action requires
the veils of illusion—that is the Hamlet Doctrine
[*die Hamletlehre*—or "to action belongs the being-
encompassed, or being-veiledness through illusion"
(*das Umschleiertsein durch die Illusion*)] not that
cheap wisdom of Jack the Dreamer who reflects too
much and, as it were, from an excess of possibilities
does not get around to action. Not reflection, no—
true knowledge, the insight into the horrible truth,
outweighs any motive for action, both in Hamlet
and in the Dionysian man.

Now no comfort avails anymore; longing
transcends a world after death; existence is negated
along with its glittering reflection in the gods or
in an immortal beyond. Conscious of the truth
he has once seen, man now sees everywhere only
the horror or absurdity of existence; now he
understands what is symbolic in Ophelia's fate;
now he understands the wisdom of the sylvan god,
Silenus: he is nauseated or disgusted [or "it disgusts
him," *es ekelt ihn*].

Here, when the danger [*Gefahr*] to his will is
greatest, *art* approaches as a saving [or redeeming,
rescuing (*rettende*)] sorceress, expert at healing.
She alone knows how to turn these nauseous or
disgusting thoughts [*Ekelgedanken*] about the
horror or absurdity of existence into notions with
which one can live: these are the *sublime* as the
artistic taming of the horrible and the *comic* as the
artistic discharge of nausea or disgust [*Ekel*]. The
satyric chorus of the dithyramb is the saving deed
of Greek art: faced with the intermediary world of
these Dionysian companions, the feelings described
here exhausted themselves.[11]

What is Nietzsche saying? The surprising initial claim is that the ecstasy of the Dionysian state, with its rupture of Apollinian boundaries and its transgression of the *principium individuationis,* is not just an affirmation of life, which is Nietzsche's main argument in *The Birth of Tragedy.* Nietzsche here seems to be acknowledging that the Dionysian is also the introduction of a kind of *lethargy* into the organism, a kind of lassitude or languor whereby we leave the everyday behind and fall into a forgetfulness of the world.[12] We could obviously link this lethargy to Freud's early formulation of the death drive in *Beyond the Pleasure Principle,* which is the introduction of a kind of inertia, or brake system, into the human organism as some regression to the origins of life—namely death. The penultimate narcissism. Life is a detour for an organism that came from nothing and will soon return to nothing. We might also link lethargy back to the slowness and inertia of *acedia,* discussed in part 1 in relation to Benjamin: the sin of sloth.

This lethargy is incarnated in various female characters in tragedy, from Aeschylus's Cassandra to Ibsen's Hedda Gabler. But the key figure is the glorious Phaedra as she appears in Euripides, Seneca, and most powerfully of all, in Racine. Phaedra wanders onstage complaining about the weight of her robes and the braiding in her hair. Her first action, in Racine's stage direction, is to sit down, *elle s'assied.* Phaedra cannot even bear the weight of her body. Languor or lethargy, we might say, weighs one down and makes one a question to oneself: to be or not to be. In Phaedra's case, her experience of languor occurs when she finds herself enchained to her incestuous desire for her stepson, Hippolytus, which is the same venial desire that her

mother felt in her monstrous coupling with the Mino-
taur. Phaedra's desire burns beneath her lethargy, breathless in her languor. Indeed, its very nearness renders her
unable to catch her breath.[13]

The extraordinary thought in our passage from *The
Birth of Tragedy* is that when we come back from this
lethargic immersion in oblivion with a sudden return to
consciousness, then we experience *Ekel*, a nausea or disgust with existence, a feeling of revulsion at the point-
lessness of existence, an ascetic and will-negating mood
or attunement (*Stimmung*). *Ekel* is a concept found elsewhere in Nietzsche. For example, in *Thus Spoke Zarathustra*, it is the counterpart of love, and Zarathustra
speaks of *der grosse Ekel* (the great disgust) and *die grosse
Liebe* (the great love). In "The Convalescent," just prior
to the first formulation of the thought of eternal return,
Zarathustra screams out:

> *Heil mir! Du kommst—ich höre dich! Mein Abgrund
> redet, meine letze Tiefe habe ich an's Licht gestülpt!*
> *Heil mir! Heran! Gieb die Hand—ha! Lass!
> Haha!—Ekel, Ekel, Ekel—wehe mir!*
> (Heal me! You are coming—I hear you! My abyss
> *speaks*, I have turned my final depth into the light!
> Heal me! Come here! Give me your hand—ha!
> Don't! Haha!—Disgust, disgust, disgust—woe is
> me!*

*Alternative Brooklyn translation of *wehe mir!* = *oi vey!*

Ekel is a word with a wide range of connotations,
including repulsion and revulsion, and it is important
to keep in mind the link to aesthetic judgments of taste,
or *gustus*, which gives us the "gust" in "dis-gust," the ill
wind in the soft-flapping sails of revulsion. Dis-gust
is an aesthetic judgment of dis-taste. Moving between

oral and anal, it is the emotion of aversion that is the opposite of gustatory pleasure. We might ask, very generally, what is it that disgusts us? From Boileau's 1674 translation of Longinus onward to Burke and Kant, we are familiar with the aesthetics of the sublime and the beautiful, but what of an aesthetics of disgust?[14]

Some say that what disgusts us is the presence of death in life, which explains our reaction to a rotting corpse or revulsion at a random, decaying body part. This claim would also explain our horror at those paranormal phenomena that refuse to respect the line between life and death, such as ghosts. But thinking of Hamlet, it would be untrue to claim that the ghost disgusts him. Neither do corpses seem to have much effect, as he coolly lugs the guts of Polonius into "the neighbor room" at the end of the brutal scene with his mother. And although Hamlet puts down Yorick's skull because it smells bad—"And smelt so? Pah!"—the skull evokes no disgust. It is rather the occasion for a little nostalgia for childhood revels—"He hath borne me on his back a thousand times"—and for a series of increasingly dark gags: "Where be your gibes now? . . . Not one now, to mock your own grinning? Quite chap-fallen?"

Hamlet's true object of disgust is not the chap with the fallen chops but is revealed in his following words. He comically instructs Yorick's bony cranium to "get to my lady's chamber" where she will "paint an inch thick" of makeup, sarcastically adding, "Make her laugh at that." What disgusts Hamlet is the occupant of his lady's chamber—namely female sexuality, whether in the form of the debased Ophelia or the degraded Gertrude. With Ophelia, during the scene when he repeatedly tells her to go to a nunnery, Hamlet makes another cosmetic reference: "God has given you one face and you make yourselves another." But his great disgust, his *grosse Ekel,* occurs in the awful linguistic violence of the scene with Gertrude just before the final appearance of the ghost. With Gertrude begging him to say no more, Hamlet screams:

> . . . But to live
> In the rank sweat of an enseamèd bed,
> Stewed in corruption, honeying and making love
> Over the nasty sty.

Hamlet is not truly disgusted by any real object, like a stinking corpse or rotting herring, but by the *idea* of the sickly sweet and semened sty of a marital bed where the bloated, suilline king fucks his mother like a sow. In other words, what disgusts Hamlet is not the materiality of an object but the ideality of fantasy in the form of the primal scene. Perhaps this follows Freud, for whom disgust is always disgust with a desire that is inevitably incestuous. Disgust, along with shame and guilt, are the prime defenses erected against desire forming a wall or barrier against incest.

Who Asked You to Swallow Men Like Oysters, Prince Hamlet?

DISGUST, NIETZSCHE SAYS in the passage above, can be borne or transformed in two ways, as the sublime and the comic, which are both variations on the effect of the satyric chorus of Attic tragedy; they are both forms of what psychoanalysts call sublimation: the transformation of passion. Beyond any question of a rebirth of tragedy, whether in his early Wagnerizing and Germanizing or his late Latinized insistence on a Dionysian future of music, Nietzsche's thought here is that art serves to reveal the essential lethargy of existence and to save us from the nausea or disgust that we feel when we're faced with it. This can be both risibly comic and tragically sublime or, perhaps more accurately, tragic-comic, which is of course how Beckett describes *Waiting for Godot,* where nothing happens twice, or almost nothing.

This is where we would like to go into Nietzsche's brief but brilliant reading of *Hamlet,* what he calls—and we tip our cap in his direction—*die Hamletlehre,* the Hamlet Doctrine. It turns on the dialectic of knowledge and action. Hamlet, for Nietzsche, resembles someone who has looked into the Dionysian urinal of being, the *Ur-Ein,* the primal unity. And this knowledge leads to disgust with action. Why? Because, he says, action can change nothing about the "eternal essence" (*ewigen Wesen*) of things, and it is either laughable or humiliating that someone like Hamlet should be asked to put right a world that is out of joint. We might recall Hamlet's remarks about, first, Denmark being a prison and, second, the world being a prison. To quote a melancholic Danish heir to Hamlet, Lars von Trier, "Nature is Satan's church."

Here is the axiomatic statement of *die Hamletlehre:* knowledge kills action, and to action there has to belong illusion or what we might now call sublimation as an act of playing with illusion, animating it with desire. Action is only possible where there is illusion, a proposition that would make any of us, believers in science and objective reality that we like to be, deeply uncomfortable. But this is what is truly radical about the Hamlet Doctrine. In Aeschylus's *Prometheus Bound*—and the image of Prometheus unbinding himself was the image on the frontispiece to the first edition of *The Birth of Tragedy*—when the captive Titan is asked what he gave human beings apart from fire and technology, Prometheus adds that he gave human beings the capacity for blind hope as a way of forestalling doom. Once you have seen into the heart of things, the heart of darkness, then why do anything? It is not an excess of reflection that kills the possibility of action. It is not that Hamlet is paralyzed and dithers this way and that like a typical obsessional neurotic. It is not that Hamlet cannot make up his mind. Not at all.

When we have what Nietzsche calls "true knowledge" (*wahre Erkenntnis*), or an insight into the cruel and horrible truth, all motivation for action evaporates. We *know* that action will accomplish precisely nothing. At this point, no comfort avails us anymore, certainly no Apollinian comfort of the beautiful dream world of illusion, what Nietzsche calls the *schöne Schein,* the lovely all-things-shining of the universe—the Terrence Malick moment. No, Nietzsche insists, we know that illusion is illusion, and we reject it. He adds that we can also certainly find no solace in life after death, an immortal beyond or some other divine comfort. No, all we see is the horror and absurdity of being. We are disgusted. Why do anything? As Nietzsche says of Hamlet, the effect of contact with horror is that *es ekelt ihn*—"life disgusts him." Nietzsche adds that the Hamlet inside all of us, the doomed person inside all of us, understands the wisdom of Silenus—"not to be born is best. Second best, die soon"—that one can find at the end of Sophocles's *Oedipus Coloneos*. Hamlet's inaction is caused not by a lack of energy but by the knowledge that action is futile.

It is not that Nietzsche was particularly enamored of Hamlet, either the play or the persona. In a section of *The Gay Science* from 1882 entitled "In Praise of Shakespeare," Nietzsche makes clear his view that *Julius Caesar* is Shakespeare's finest play because of its depiction of Brutus (oddly, the roots of the names Brutus and Hamlet, Amlodi and Amleth, mean "stupid"). He writes,

> I could not say anything more beautiful in praise of Shakespeare *as a human being* than this: he believed in Brutus and did not cast one speck of suspicion upon this type of virtue. It is to him that he devoted his best tragedy—it is still called by the wrong name.[15]

Julius Caesar should have been entitled *Brutus,* and maybe *Hamlet* could have been called *Stupid.* Nietzsche goes on, "What is all of Hamlet's melancholy compared to that of Brutus?" This rather dim view of Hamlet continues later in *The Gay Science,* where Nietzsche claims that Hamlet's misanthropy—"Man delights not me"—flows from an all too greedy love of man and "cannibalism." Nietzsche asks the oddly molluscan rhetorical question, "Who asked you to swallow men like Oysters, Prince Hamlet?"

Lest one think that the passage from *The Birth of Tragedy* is some youthful blip, in his final period of manic creativity—in *Ecce Homo*—there is a curious return to Nietzsche's earlier understanding of the figure of Hamlet. In "Why I Am So Clever," just after a brief reprise of his conviction that the ill-named *Julius Caesar* is Shakespeare's best play, he writes:

> I know of no more heartrending reading-matter than Shakespeare: what must a person have suffered if he needs to be a clown that badly!—Is Hamlet *understood*? It is not doubt, but *certainty* that drives you mad. . . . But you need to be profound, abyss, philosopher to feel that way. . . . We are all *afraid* of the truth.[16]

To borrow a favorite, cowlike word of Nietzsche's, this passage merits careful rumination (*wiederkäuen*). Echoing the long passage from *The Birth of Tragedy,* Hamlet's experience is not characterized by doubt but by certainty. It is not that he doesn't know but that he suffers from an excess of knowledge through his contact with the Dionysian void. It is the certainty of this access to the truth that drives Hamlet mad.

Hamlet, then, is a philosopher, a creature of the depths, one who looks into the abyss and feels fear but still feels obliged and even compelled to look. What is clear from the passage in *Ecce Homo* is that Nietzsche's understanding of *Hamlet* doesn't change from the beginning to the end of his work and might arguably provide a way of framing his entire work. What we mean is that the abyss that Nietzsche finds in *Hamlet* is one that he also seems to find in himself. The question "Is Hamlet *understood*?" is the same question that he ceaselessly poses to himself in his late work, particularly in the final, frantic pages of *Ecce Homo,* which ends with the words—almost Nietzsche's final words—"Have I been understood? *Dionysos against the crucified one.*"[17]

To turn Nietzsche's interpretation of *Hamlet* against himself in what we might also call "an attempt at self-criticism," it might be said: we know of no more heartrending reading matter than Nietzsche. What must he have suffered to need to be a buffoon to this extent? Might we not ponder whether the Dionysian Nietzsche identifies himself with Hamlet in his opposition to the crucified Christ? Might not the melancholy and misanthropy that he finds in Hamlet be that abyss that he recognizes in himself? Might it not be the irresistible oceanic undertow of negation that pulls against Nietzsche's otherwise relentless assertion of affirmation and that threatens to submerge and drown him?

Nietzsche, like Hamlet, is a man that knows too much. And disgust would here be the Hamletized response to existence that he continually tries to choke down: "*Disgust* at man is my danger."[18] Maybe this explains Nietzsche's mad antics, like writing an autobiography like *Ecce Homo* with megalomaniac chapter titles like "Why I Am So Wise," "Why I Am So Clever," "Why I Write Such Excellent Books," and "Why I Am a Destiny." Can he be serious? Perhaps the only thing to do when one has looked into the abyss of suffering is to become a buffoon. We all fear the truth.

As he writes in the final pages of *Ecce Homo,* "I don't want to be a saint, and would rather be a buffoon. . . . Perhaps I am a buffoon."[19] In section 3 of "Why I Am So Wise," in a passage deleted by his dreadful proto-Nazi sister, Nietzsche jokes that "the most profound objection against 'eternal recurrence,' my truly *abyssal* thought, is always my mother and sister." Everything can return *apart from them.* For Nietzsche, it is the most extreme sign of vulgarity to feel oneself related to one's parents. After confessing that Richard Wagner was the person most closely related to him, he adds, Hamlet-like, anticipating Freud, "The rest is silence."[20]

Through the Ghost of the Unquiet Father, the Image of the Unliving Son Looks Forth

NIETZSCHE'S THOUGHT OF the vulgarity of familial relations finds its echo in Joyce's astonishing trumping of all Shakespeare criticism in *Ulysses*. Joyce's mode of hyperacceleration seems to outrun the very possibility of interpretation, effortlessly folding the multifarious threads of scholarship into this work. Although *Ulysses* is a rumination on *Hamlet* from beginning to end, "Scylla and Charybdis" is the famous chapter set in the National Library where Stephen Dedalus and his cohort debate the scholarship that tries to pinpoint Shakespeare's identity in relation to his work, with Stephen increasingly collapsing into the figure of Hamlet himself (and Leopold Bloom, who creeps ghostlike into the library at the end of the chapter, folding into Hamlet Senior).

Stephen subsumes the questions that haunt *Hamlet* into the very question of haunting that accompanies all life, all creation. For Joyce, *Hamlet* is the Irish play par excellence: full of usurpers, exiles, the dead, the guilty, and the dispossessed. *Ulysses* forms around a play between Stephen Dedalus—his mother dead, his God dead, his father renounced, whose country has the shape of a vast question mark under the incurious thumbprint of British imperial rule—and Bloom, the cuckold Jew, the exile without a fatherland or a son. *Ulysses* is about the impossibility of home rule. Bloom cannot rule his home, and Molly screws other men in his bed. Stephen, "a horrible example of free thought," is still the cringing servant of two masters, the priest and the king that he has to kill, but cannot. "Home also I cannot go," he says.

For Stephen, *Hamlet* is a ghost story, and the morsel of Shakespeare lore that he finds most haunting is the idea that the Bard played the ghost, the murdered father. After the death of his father in 1601 and the death of his son, Hamnet, in 1596, Shakespeare was playing the ghost of a father at the moment that he was no longer a father and no longer a son:

> The play begins . . . it is the ghost, the king, a king and no king, and the player is Shakespeare who has studied *Hamlet* all the years of his life which were not vanity in order to play the part of the spectre. He speaks the words to Burbage. . . .
> *Hamlet, I am thy father's spirit*
> bidding him list. To a son he speaks, the son of his soul, the prince, young Hamlet and to the son of his body, Hamnet Shakespeare, who has died in Stratford that his namesake may live forever.

What Joyce is doing, however, in using this structure to shape the dramatic action of *Ulysses* is taking these themes a step further. What is a father? What is a son? These two questions need to be scrutinized before any establishment of the biographical "facts." Indeed, Joyce is tracing the question of kinship, both physical and metaphysical. Isn't this really the question of *Hamlet?*

Joyce is constantly playing with the question of creation, which he turns into the question of the father, of paternity. The question of the father and the latter's identity or con-substantiality with the son organizes theological debates within early Christianity, as Joyce well knew. *Mater semper certa est pater numquam.* What leaps must be made in order for a father to become a father as such? And what of the mother's certainty? Is that not also a curse? It suits Joyce that Anne Hathaway was thought to be a viperous older wife who had ensnared Shakespeare with her pregnancy. As the famous joke goes, "If others have their will Anne hath a way. By cock, she was to blame." So follows all of Shakespeare's blather in the sonnets about desire and the dark lady.

Stephen's friend, Russell—like us—is impatient with all this "prying" into the life of a great man, "the speculation of schoolboys for schoolboys" (like the fact that, in Trieste in 1912 to 1913, shortly before beginning to write *Ulysses,* Joyce gave a series of twelve lectures on *Hamlet,* the contents of which are now lost). For Russell, such speculation leaves out the place where words touch "formless, spiritual essences." But Stephen will not be seduced by any such Walter Pater–esque Platonism. What is indeed banal about psychobiography finds its negative dialectical complement in this ridiculous aesthetic romanticism. The question for Stephen is what has been sundered in a life, for only then can we know what might be reconciled. The Scylla and Charybdis of psychobiographical reductionism and romanticism are the twin obstacles:

> If you want to know what are the events which cast their shadow over the hell of time of *King Lear, Othello, Hamlet, Troilus and Cressida,* look to see when and how the shadow lifts.

He continues:

He goes back, weary of the creation he has piled up to hide him from himself, an old dog licking an old sore. . . . He is a ghost, a shadow now, the wind by Elsinore's rocks or what you will, the sea's voice, a voice heard only in the heart of him who is the substance of his shadow, the son consubstantial with the father.

What is sundered, then, is the relation between father and son, creator and created, for a son's "growth is his father's decline, his youth his father's envy, his friend his father's enemy." Perhaps, Stephen ponders, this is the real truth of original sin—a cycle of violence that runs between infanticide to patricide. Only a ghost, a dead father, a spectral fiction, it seems, can be consubstantial with a son—a whisper in a shadow heart.

Paternity, Joyce declares, is a necessary evil, a legal family fiction, as vulgar as Nietzsche imagined. Stephen asks, "Who is the father of any son that any son should love him or he any son?" What links father and son in nature is "An instant of blind rut"—no more. Paternity is not a physical state as much as what Stephen calls a "mystical estate, an apostolic succession, from only begetter to only begotten." This is the strange truth of Stephen's Hamlet Doctrine, summarized by Judge Eglinton: that Shakespeare "is the ghost and the prince. He is all in all." But if paternity is a ghostly fiction for Joyce, if it is nothing and springs from nothing—all is exilic banishment from the heart and the home—then perhaps reconciliation takes on a new sense. Namely, the one that Shakespeare-Hamlet-Joyce gives:

Well: if the father who has not a son be not a father can the son who has not a father be a son? When Rutlandbaconsouthhamptonshakespeare or another poet of the same name in the comedy of errors wrote *Hamlet* he was not the father of his own son merely but, being no more a son, he was and felt himself the father of all his race, the father of his own grandfather, the father of his unborn grandson who, by the same token, never was born for nature.

We are united by this nothing—a king and a beggar but variable service, as Hamlet says—Hamlet *père* and Hamlet *fils* buried by gravediggers, all in all. The only universal is in the nothing that binds us together. We find ourselves on that Joycean knife's edge between nihilism and *creatio ex nihilo,* man and God, individual and universal, Nobodaddy and Everyman, writing in the black space between dreams. As Stephen says at the end of his interpretation of *Hamlet,* "I believe, O Lord, help my unbelief."

The mystical consubstantiality of Bloom and Dedalus finally transpires after midnight outside the brothels of nighttown after Stephen has been beaten senseless. "JewGreek is greekjew. Extremes meet." This occasions the rhapsodic, ghostly apparition of Bloom's dead son—Rudy—and his rather-excessive paternalism toward Stephen. But Stephen refuses this new mystical father and, after urinating together in the garden back at Bloom's house, he leaves. He does not know where he is going. There will be no reconciliation, no happy ending, no homoerotic union through submission to the father-prophet. Perhaps, however, this no, this nothing ending, gives itself over to something else. Like Antigone pushing her way past Oedipus and Hamlet, Molly Bloom's sultry soliloquy—the pure unpunctured and unpunctuated flow of her desire—emerges as a new feminine voice of affirmation. Yes I said Yes I will Yes.

I *Want* to Be a *Woman*

WHY DOES NIETZSCHE say that Hamlet now understands what is symbolic in Ophelia's fate? What exactly
is symbolic in Ophelia's fate? First, what is her fate?
Ophelia kills herself after having become psychotic
because Hamlet, the man she loved and who loved
her once, succumbs to what Adorno calls "The Hamlet Syndrome," debasing her violently, and killing her
father. Nietzsche seems to be insinuating that Ophelia
kills herself because she sees the horror and absurdity of
existence and cannot bear it. In this she is much more
courageous than Hamlet, who can neither kill himself,
although that is his first thought in the play ("Had not
the Everlasting fixed his canon 'gainst self-slaughter"),
nor can he kill Claudius, the usurper king. We might
say that Nietzsche sees *Hamlet* as a two-headed play
of failed love. Both Ophelia and Hamlet see the same
thing, but where Hamlet dithers and feigns madness,
Ophelia erupts in a sexualized psychosis that leads unre-
mittingly to her self-chosen demise. In this, she exhibits an Antigone-like unwillingness to give way to her
desire and unites with the object world—nature—in
her muddy, beautiful death.

In this connection, we'd like to turn briefly to
Heiner Müller's *Hamletmaschine* (and note the
repeated initials: *H.M.*) from 1977, what he calls "the
shrunken head of the Hamlet tragedy." In truth, it is a

double shrunken-headed tragedy whose main character is arguably Ophelia. Müller acknowledged that the character of Ophelia is to some extent based on Ulrike Meinhof, the cofounder of the Red Army Faction, who hanged herself in her cell, most Antigone-like, in May 1976. The play begins with Hamlet announcing himself in the past tense—"I was Hamlet." When Ophelia appears, her heart as a clock, she says, "I am Ophelia." If, for Nietzsche, whatever is symbolic in Ophelia's fate provokes the affect of disgust, then the latter spills all over *Hamletmaschine:*

> Choking with disgust, I shake my fist at myself . . . Television the daily disgust Disgust . . . Since thine is nothingness Disgust . . . Of the lies which are believed / By the liars and nobody else / Disgust / Of the lies which are believed Disgust . . . By their struggle for positions votes bank accounts Disgust . . . In the solitude of airports I breathe again I am / A privileged person My Disgust / Is a privilege / Protected by torture / Barbed wire prisons . . .

For Müller's Hamlet, thoughts are like lesions in the brain, and because of this intense disgust he declares, *"Ich will eine Maschine sein,"* "I want to be a machine." The only escape from horror is into thoughtless automatism. Of course, Shakespeare's Hamlet refers to himself as a machine in the final line of his letter to Ophelia that Polonius reads out to Claudius in order to confirm his dumb love hypothesis:

> Thine evermore, most dear lady, whilst
> this machine is to him, HAMLET.[21]

Müller brings out brilliantly the Nietzschean misanthropy in the character of Hamlet and also his twisted misogyny:

Women should be sewed up—a world without mothers. We could butcher each other in peace and quiet . . . My mother the bride. Her breasts a rosebed, her womb the snakepit . . . I'll change you back into a virgin mother, so your king will have a bloodwedding. A MOTHER'S WOMB IS NOT A ONE-WAY STREET.

Ophelia asks Hamlet before bursting into laughter, "Do you want to eat my heart, Hamlet?" To which he replies, "I want to be a woman." At which point, Hamlet travesties in Ophelia's clothes, she plasters him with makeup, and Hamlet poses as a whore before dancing wildly with Horatio—wish fulfillment, indeed.

Of course, there is a certain tradition of interpretation, dating back at least to Edward P. Vining's 1881 *The Mystery of Hamlet,* which sees Hamlet not as "the masculine type of human perfection . . . but also the feminine type."[22] This leads him to the conclusion that "this womanly man might be in very deed a woman,"[23] which explains, for Vining, Hamlet's intense attachment to Horatio, the vituperativeness of his relations with women in the play (all women are bitches or whores, it would appear), and his physical weakness in the duel with Laertes (really?). As ever, Joyce is way ahead of us. Early in Bloom's perambulation, he pauses outside the Gaiety Theatre and reflects on the performance of the American actress Mrs. Bandman Palmer: "*Hamlet* she played last night. Male impersonator. Perhaps he was a woman. Why Ophelia committed suicide?"

For Müller, wanting to be a woman on Hamlet's part has little to do with gender confusion. Hamlet wants to eat Ophelia's heart because it "weeps" his "tears." Ophelia is a heroine, and Hamlet is an Opheliac. He wants to be a woman, for she is the one who speaks, who has the will to die, who has left her prison. Hamlet says:

> My drama if it still would happen, would happen in the time of an uprising. . . . Oosing word-slime. . . . my drama didn't happen. The script has been lost. . . . I go home and kill the time, at one with my undivided self.

Hamlet belongs to the "university of the dead," disgusted and dressed up in makeup or his father's suit of armor. He walks around smashing false idols—Marx, Lenin, Mao, ice and snow. He stumbles "from hole to hole towards the final hole," a bloated bloodhound, a listless philosopher. Ophelia exhibits anything but this kind of cowardice:

> I am Ophelia. The one the river didn't keep. The woman dangling from the rope. The woman with her arteries cut open. The woman with the over-dose. SNOW ON HER LIPS. The woman with her head in the gas stove. Yesterday I stopped killing myself. I'm alone with my breasts my thighs my womb. I smash the tools of my captivity, the chair the table the bed. I destroy the battlefield that was my home . . . I set fire to my prison. I throw my clothes into the fire. I wrench the clock that was my heart out of my breast. I walk the street clothed in my blood.

Ophelia tears out her heart, bleeds, shatters herself at the limit between life and death, a figure of sacrifice without redemption, who, despite this, still has the will to act.

In Müller's *Hamletmaschine,* Ophelia—seated motionless in a wheelchair, wrapped in white gauze and surrounded by fish, debris, and dead bodies—is the last character left onstage. Ventriloquizing the frighteningly strident persona of Electra, Ophelia's final words are:

> Long live hate and contempt, rebellion and death. When she walks through your bedrooms carrying butcher knives you'll know the truth.

I want to be Ophelia. And so do I.

Absolutely-Too-Much

Allow us a speculative parenthesis and a modest proposal. In Kant's *Critique of the Power of Judgment,* he makes a passing but suggestive set of distinctions among the beautiful, the sublime, and the monstrous. The beautiful is the free play of the imagination and understanding, when everything seems to hang together, rather like driving a humming-engined expensive German car through the California desert. The sublime is what is refractory to the formal harmony of the experience of beauty, something formless, indefinite, and mighty but still containable within the realm of the aesthetic. For Kant, the sublime is "the almost-too-much" and is distinguished from the monstrous understood as "the absolutely-too-much." That which is monstrous defeats our capacity for conceptual comprehension. Kant simply asserts that the monstrous has no place in the realm of aesthetics. The great aesthetic danger is the moment when the tamed terror of sublimity—the Alps or Mount Snowdon for the English Romantics—might tip over into the monstrous. Indeed, in the founding text of philosophical aesthetics, *Poetics,* Aristotle makes an analogous gesture when he makes a distinction between the fearful (*to phoberon*), which has a legitimate place within tragedy, and the monstrous (*to teratodes*), which has no place at all.

But what might art be when it exceeds the relative

comfort of the almost-too-much of the sublime or the fearful and moves toward the absolutely-too-much of the monstrous? What happens when the uncontainable can't be contained? When art bears at its core something unbearable? At this point, art becomes antiart and we experience discomfort—what Bruce Nauman perhaps had in mind when he declared that art should be a blow to the back of the neck. We would argue that what has been happening for the past century or so in various arts and media as a way of dealing with our presentiment of the unbearable pressure of reality, however we want to capture that experience—the shocking trauma of the First World War, poetry after Auschwitz is barbarism, or whatever—has been the experimentation with what we might call *an art of the monstrous.* Examples proliferate here, from Artaud's Theater of Cruelty to Bataille's holy disgust to Hermann Nitsch's blood orgies and the theater of Heiner Müller or, more recently, Sarah Kane, even through to that most jaded and overworked of academic tropes: the abject.

If we look back at much of what is most radical and interesting in the art of the last century, we can see that we are no longer dealing with the sublime or indeed with art as the possibility of aesthetic sublimation but with an art of *de-sublimation* that attempts to adumbrate the monstrous, the uncontainable, the unreconciled, that which is unbearable in our experience of reality.

Here is our modest proposal: beyond endless video montages and the cold mannerist obsessionality of the taste for appropriation and reenactment that has become hegemonic in the art world, the heart of any artistic response to the present should perhaps be the cultivation of the monstrous and its concomitant affect—

disgust. Disgust here can be thought of as the visceral register of a monstrosity that can no longer be excluded from the realm of the aesthetic, as it was for Aristotle and Kant, but should be its arrhythmic heart, its hot, volatile, and distasteful core.

Perhaps Nietzsche's wild idea of his own posthumous birth might be interpreted as the thought that art must now fix its stare unblinkingly at the monstrous, the unbearable, the unreconciled, and the insanely troubling. The disgust that we feel might not simply repulse or repel us. It might also wake us up. This is the force of the uncontainable that we find in tragedy, whether ancient or modern. The disgust that we feel might not just destroy us. We don't have to follow Ophelia into a watery grave. We think it is a question of how we think through and deploy the essential violence of art and perhaps understand art as violence against the violence of reality, a violence that presses back against the violence of reality, which is perhaps the task of tragic poetry in a state that is rotten and in a time that is out of joint.

We think here of Francis Bacon. When he was asked to reflect on the purported violence of his painting, Bacon said: "When talking about the violence of paint, it's nothing to do with the violence of war. It's to do with an attempt to remake the violence of reality." He goes on:

> We nearly always live through screens—a screened existence. And I sometimes think, when people say my work looks violent, that I have been able to clear away one or two of the veils or screens.

Existence seems to us ever more screened and distanced. This is the risk of a shallow shadow world whose ideological pancake patina is an empty empathy for a suffering that we do nothing to stop and everything to abet in our passivity, dispersal, and narcissism. None of us is free of this. Maybe art, in its essential violence, can tear away one or two of these screens. Maybe then we'll begin to see. We do not see as we are seen because we are wrapped in a screen. Art might unwrap us a little through its violence.

But what is it that disgusts us? Ay, there's the rub. The problem with disgust is that it is a moving limit. What outrages one generation—Bacon, say—becomes slothful banality to the next. The problem here is that art, which is meant to enable or produce some kind of experience of the real in our pushing back against it, might finally be a protection against that experience and end up as a kind of decoration. Perhaps, then, art has to become the enemy of aesthetic experience. In which case, we should become the enemies of art in order to reclaim it. Here antiart becomes true art in a constant war of position with the degeneration of art's critical potential into the Lethean waters of the contemporary.

Conclusion

O, O, O, O. Dies

CONSIDER THE END of *Hamlet*. As we all know, Hamlet's final words to Horatio are "The rest is silence," which is one final nothing in the drama. But whichever way one plays it or views it, *Hamlet* ends not with serenity, authenticity, or disinterest but farcically—like a macabre puppet show—with a huge pile of corpses. All the main protagonists are alive, disputing and drinking, having placed their bets on the sword fight, and then, in the space of fifty-six lines, they all drop stone dead. Indeed, Hamlet tells us he is dead three times before he eventually croaks. When all is said and done, it is Hamlet's *inauthenticity* that most intrigues us and that we'd like to underline in closing. Hamlet never overcomes the division within himself in the name of some Stoical serenity underwritten by an appeal to a vague divinity. When he tries to apologize to Laertes in the final scene of the play, he speaks in the present tense, "I *am* punished with a sore distraction." Hamlet then goes on to develop the most extraordinary self-defense by arguing that his madness entails diminished responsibility, speaking of himself in the third person:

> Was't Hamlet wronged Laertes? Never Hamlet.
> If Hamlet from himself be ta'en away,
> And when he's not himself does wrong Laertes,
> Then Hamlet does it not, Hamlet denies it.

Who does it, then? His madness. If't be so,
Hamlet is of the faction that is wronged:
His madness is poor Hamlet's enemy.

Ask yourself: are these the words of an authentic, autarchic, serene, and self-contained subject? To the very end, Hamlet lives outside himself, submitting to the will of Claudius in the rapier fight with his semblable and double, Laertes. He dies not with his own name on his lips or even the name of his father, but by lending his "dying voice" to Fortinbras. In fact, Hamlet dies with nothing on his lips, or more precisely four zeroes. In the Folio edition, what would appear to be Hamlet's final words are followed by "O, O, O, O. *Dies.*"

To push this a little further—doubtless too far— consider the tragicomedy of the final lines of *Hamlet*. After the main characters have dropped like flies in an almost Monty Python–esque manner, Horatio is the last man standing. Right on cue (and just too late), Fortinbras and the English ambassadors turn up onstage. Seeing the pile of corpses, Fortinbras wonders out loud what kind of death festival this might be:

O proud Death,
What feast is toward in thine eternal cell,
That thou so many princes at a shot
So bloodily hast struck?

In other words: Gosh, what a lot of corpses! It gets even stranger when the English ambassador declares that Rosencrantz and Guildenstern are dead. To paraphrase, he says that they were killed as instructed, but the person who instructed them to do so has unfortunately also been killed. He then rather rudely asks,

"Where should we have our thanks." In other words, who is going to pay us for our dirty work? Horatio, gesturing toward Hamlet's corpse, declares in a rather-macabre manner, "Not from his mouth." Dead men don't speak. Lest we forget, death is that undiscovered country from where no traveler returns. Except in *Hamlet,* of course, where dead men do speak and death would appear to be something more congested than a one-way street.

Horatio then assumes a certain regal power and authority, giving orders that the bodies be placed "High on a stage," as if in a theater. Warming to his task, Horatio teases the Norwegian king-to-be with the goriness of his tale:

> So, shall you hear
> Of carnal, bloody and unnatural acts,
> Of accidental judgments, casual slaughters,
> Of deaths put on by cunning and forced cause . . .
> All this can I
> Truly deliver.

Fortinbras is excited, as young Americans say, "Let us haste to hear it," but then immediately changes the topic to the rather more important matter of his election to the crown of Denmark. Horatio adds:

> Of that I shall also have cause to speak,
> And from his mouth whose voice will draw on
> more.

But wait a moment! It seems that the dead Hamlet *will* speak after all, ventriloquized or pneumatically animated by Horatio as puppet master, or spymaster, as we hypothesized above. The dead Hamlet's speech will be "more" than when he was alive. Hamlet's speech is more than nothing only when he is nothing, as if following the strange logic of Freud's *Totem and Taboo* that only a dead father speaks and has the force of law. And the dead Hamlet must speak because his voice "will draw on more," it will be more influential with the "more"—namely, the rabble, the muddied people, who are prone to the seduction of political intrigue and falsehood. Without further delay, and note the repetition of the appeal to "more," Horatio decides it is politically crucial that the true tragical history of Hamlet be:

> . . . Presently performed
> Even while men's minds are wild, lest more mischance
> On plots and errors happen.

With these words, Hamlet's body is borne "like a soldier to the stage" by four captains, but the other corpses are also to be transported and "placèd to the view." Fortinbras gives the final command: "Take up the bodies."

Is this whole scene not truly bizarre? *Hamlet* ends with Horatio making good on his promise to tell Hamlet's story. And he does so immediately for political reasons in order to forestall any error and guarantee the swift election of Fortinbras as king of Denmark. So, *Hamlet* ends with the promise to perform the tragedy of Hamlet. Like *The Mouse-trap,* then, *The Tragicall Historie of Hamlet, Prince of Denmarke* is a play within a play, the truth of which will be told by Horatio in a further play acted before Fortinbras, the English ambassadors, and the muddied multitude of Denmark. We might want to call it *Hamlet II.* The difference this time is that all the actors will be dead. Horatio promises to act out the tragedy of Hamlet with all the bodies set high onstage and on view. More than mere

Trauerspiel, Hamlet II will be a corpse drama, a piece of degenerate agitprop with the dead Hamlet in the lead somehow being dragged around by Horatio, who will speak his lines and presumably the lines of all the other dead actors. Perhaps it's a good thing that only the three different versions of *Hamlet I* are extant.

I Will Gain Nothing but My Shame

IF *Hamlet* is, in a deep sense, a play about nothing that shows not beautiful authentic disinterestedness but the scope and scale of our ugly inauthentic interests, then what follows from this? We talked above about cultivating a disposition of skeptical openness, which sounds very nice, but is that it? The first thing to insist upon is that Shakespeare is not like Guinness. It is not just good for you. If we think we know what the good is and that *Hamlet* confirms us in such knowledge, then we are not experiencing the dramatic complexity and sheer moral ambiguity of the tragedy. In our view, the problem with the humanist line of criticism that sees *Hamlet* in terms of an ethics of authenticity is that it too readily forecloses the experience of shame in relation to the play. For us, at its deepest, this is a play about shame, the nothing that is the experience of shame.

Shame peppers and punctuates the play when an excess or lack in action makes itself felt as such.[1] Hamlet accuses Gertrude of having no shame, "O shame, where is thy blush," and then wallows in his own when he sees what he imagines as twenty thousand men going to their death for nothing, for a trick of fame, for shame. Laertes even calls shame a woman who says what she will, having given up on the customs of nature. Shame, from one end of the play to the other, is the affect that accompanies being out of joint, a wobble in the projector or a shaking of the frame. It does not have the structure of intentional consciousness directed with clarity and distinctness toward an object that it reveals. Rather, shame moves in the opposite direction. Its subject is exterior to us. It evokes something blushingly powerful but opaque. It moves on the outside across surfaces like fire in grass. It is a veiled and veiling affect.

One might even say that it is the affect of the veil contra Nietzsche for whom it is disgust. Disgust emerges in Nietzsche more from having torn through the veil, having punctured it, only then to fall back into oneself. In the same way that one might say horror creeps up, violence wells up, and silence descends, disgust is reactive: yuk!!! Shame, on the other hand, in its pure externality, is more about the experience of limitation. It stops you in your tracks. It does not define an interior in revolt but limits the infinity that haunts any interiorization.

Shame, one might say, is an experience of one's most basic subjective dividedness, which perhaps first appears in the experience of being seen and seen intimately. You never look at me from the place where I see you, and what I look at is never what I want to see. Or to borrow a wonderful Greek expression from Anne Carson, "shame lies on the eyelids." What we see in tragedy after tragedy are characters who initially experience no shame, no division. They are often called tyrants, as in *Oedipus the King* (*Oidipous Tyrannos*). The tyrant—like Oedipus, Creon, or Claudius—is shameless, and tragedy might be said to provide lessons in shame. When we learn that lesson and achieve some insight, as with Oedipus, then it might cost us our sight as we pluck out our eyes, for shame. As we said above, it is not that the scales fall from our eyes, but that our eyes fall like scales. Shame is a lesson on the imbalance of all scales of measurement. To be clear, we are not recommending drowning in shame. We need not too much of it, but just enough.

Philosophy and psychoanalysis have traditionally tended to couple shame with guilt in a hierarchy that privileges the latter over the former. It is said that guilt is the achievement of modernity, where a fully inwardized subject fights with the pangs and scruples of bad conscience. Modernity is the move inward that takes place through the internalization of the law. Guilt is the endpoint in a progressivist vision of man on a path toward autonomy, authenticity, and self-determination. In this view, shame is only experienced when a wrong is seen from the outside and not when it is felt as the violation of an internal law or principle. Shame is primitive. We do not, as we hope we have made clear, follow this neat epochal division that separates the ancients from the moderns, degrading the opacity of shame in the clear light of guilt. In any case, as we showed earlier, the apex of guilt and fault, especially in *Hamlet,* can be seen as an infinite, impossible game of blame grounded in an excited revulsion with instinct, sexuality, desire, and all that is all-too-human. This dialectic of guilt and law is the finally narcissistic prison of bad conscience. But shame teaches us something else.

The political world of *Hamlet* and our own time—rotten and out of joint as it is—are stuffed full of sham shame, ham humility, and tearful, staged remorse. We might call this *shamletization.* But true shame is something else. It is something that lies on the eyelids. It is not something in you; it is on you. You are saturated by shame from the outside—"shame on you!" We lash

out against others only to have it rebound upon ourselves. It is a moment of seeing oneself from the outside in the manner of Hamlet's endless soliloquies. In
his case, the other whom he cannot kill, but whom he
desperately wants to kill, conditions his shame. We say
to ourselves, "I could die of shame," precisely because
we cannot. We have to live with this shame, as with
ourselves.

This is why shame is tied so closely to the experience of mortification—it erupts at the place where
death brings itself to bear in life, tearing us to pieces.
It is the very experience of the body's mortality. Lest
we need to be reminded by Freud, this mortified body
is condemned to die precisely because it is sexed. We
are not immortal. We cannot, like bacteria or clones,
endlessly reproduce ourselves out of ourselves. Shame
is the experience of this fallen state, the exacerbation
of a division within the self. It is something essentially
inauthentic and excessive that cannot be controlled and
that erupts like blush on one's cheeks. It appears at the
place where an intimacy is sensed but not understood,
recoiling from shame toward an act that takes cogni-
zance of human limitation—modesty, discretion, tact,
and prudence. Theater, in its best Gorgiastic deceptiveness, acts like a demonic machine that produces shame
in the spectator, who, alone in the dark, blushes or perhaps bites the carpet.

The Most Monstrous Contradiction of Love

WE'D LIKE TO DRAW this book to a close with the question of love, a question we find palpably current as if the world spoke to us about nothing else but love's impossibility. One might even claim that this is a contemporary plague. Freud did, although he traces the contemporary back to the prehistoric juncture of human civilization. For Freud, the inability to love is the discontent within civilization.

To our mind, there is a virtue in intimately linking shame and love, for it is only in the experience of self-division—close to the kind of shameful self-lacerating passion that we elevate above anything syrupy sweet—that love can enter into play. As the eros-ridden, God-hungry love of the great medieval mystic Marguerite Porete testifies: only in hacking and hewing the narrowest of cleavages in the soul can the divine whisper his words of love. The work and risk of love is an experience at the limit, our last-ditch effort at transgression or transcendence, which is why it is closer to pain than any Edenic joy it might seem to promise.

To be clear, love as we see it promises nothing. It is the very nothing of the promise, one that can only be renewed and invented anew, again and again. I love you. I love you. I love you. Even then, the possibility that love remains not only unreciprocated—I love you not—but wrapped entirely in the conceit of a self-absorbed wishful fantasy, the other merely a pawn in this repeated loop, can find no final refutation. The only proof of love may be the ease with which it can be betrayed. The experience of shame is a litmus test for the possibility of love, and theater might be seen as directed to one in the secret hope of the other.

Of course, there is wisdom in *not* writing about love. Matters can quickly degrade into sentimentality and threaten to don the illusory narcissistic garb of love-cum-bliss and self-rapture. Perhaps love is best written about in its almost absolute negation, *Hamlet* being one of the most powerful examples. As Hamlet says to Ophelia, "I could interpret between you and your love / if I could see the puppets dallying." Whether it is the painful lassitude of melancholy, the slew of obscene innuendo, the nihilistic disgust with existence, or an incestuous rage-fueled inhibition, what passes between Hamlet and Ophelia is a discourse on love in a kaleidoscopic array of negative forms: "I did love you once . . . I loved you not."

One of the secret heroes in this book, Herman Melville, turns to *Hamlet* in the one landlocked love story he wrote with the strange expectation that it would become a housewife best-seller and rescue him from almost destitute poverty. The result—*Pierre; or, The Ambiguities*—was both too weird and too radical. The hinge in the novel turns on the revelation of shame that shatters Pierre's initial naïve, almost comical, romanticism. He falls into poverty like his author. Melville approaches love through the walls of the impossibility that define it, from the confines of convention and the dull safety of a marital agreement on one side to the romantic illusions and immaturity of adolescent love on another to incestuous forbidden pleasure that is at worst a symbiosis of pure self-destruction and at best an inherited familial shame that haunts and envelops all choice. *Pierre; or, The Ambiguities* was a total flop, and it ends, like *Hamlet,* in a pile of corpses. Throwing his hands in the air, Melville writes, "Let the ambiguous procession of events reveal their own ambiguousness."

There is a psychoanalytic myth called the *lamella.* This is a word used in biology, botany, and anatomy to refer to a thin membrane or casing. Lacan used it to metaphorize the idea of a narcissitic shell, a myth employed to illustrate the stakes of love in the games of erotic passion and commitment. If we allow our desire to puncture this lamella, moving toward another, a piece of it is lost to us that we might seek to recuperate. Narcissistic love wants to get this little fragment back, to be compensated by another for having emerged from the safety of our membranous enclosure. The contract is set up: if I love you, then you must consent to give back to me what I have lost in doing so. Love becomes a system of mutual favors in which loss is ultimately avoided.

Happily, there is another way. What causes us to desire—to leave the safety of an insular, lamellar world—punctures a hole in the very heart of our being. Through the other we can come closer to what we have lost. Love makes this absence present. To love passionately is this commerce of nothings, which is why love is defined more by the little nothings whispered between lovers than any bodily union. When Hamlet says, "For God's love, let me hear," this is always spoken from within a void. "Speak to me" is a plea to no one, anyone, at the same time that it is always and only to the beloved that it is really addressed.

The disjunction at the heart of the myth of the lamella allowed Lacan to define love surrealistically as "giving what one does not have to another who doesn't want it." With the beloved I never really know if I am given back this piece of my being, whether I have for them what they seem to desire in me, or even if I encounter something beyond myself in this attempt at a radical exchange of naught. Precarious illusions, if lucky, dissipate like smoke in the atmosphere with these claims of love. Let the ambiguous procession of events reveal, to shame, their own ambiguousness. Those, it is said, that love well, can say very little about it. Is this not what makes writing about love so hazardous? Hamlet, lest we remind you, cannot love but can speak very well about a world depleted of it.

The betrayal of love is treason against the mutual conquest of illusion that lovers attempt in vain. Lovers commit to find out—to continue to find out, in fidelity—if they can breach the walls of impossibility. Finally, it is never an act in reality that destroys love. Rather, it is the betrayal of the original stakes of the commitment. One need only say, "I never gave you ought," "'tis common," "this is the very coinage of your brain," "you were deceived," "you should not have believed me." Betrayal of this kind announces itself without a single point of division, leaving the other mortified, ashamed, humiliated in the face of what is paraded before them as a brute reality. Words of betrayal are spoken in absolute bad faith. They signal a time "out of joint." It is in their tenor that most dialogue is mouthed in *Hamlet*—except, of course, for Ophelia. As the lover in *Hamlet* she is for us the play's real casualty and true tragic hero.

Love, like shame, knows something about passionately ruffling the folds in the veils of illusion to reveal a new truth—the work of a good Gorgiastic theatrocrat. As Hegel writes somewhere in a note, love is the most monstrous contradiction. It defies understanding. To love is to give what one does not have and to receive that over which one has no power. To love is to freely negate the stubbornness that is the self and to live in loyalty to an affirmation that can dissolve like morning mist with the first experience of betrayal. To be or not to be—*is* that the question? Perhaps not. Perhaps love is a negation of the being of my selfish self that binds itself to naught, to little nothings in the hope of receiving back something that exceeds my power, my ability, my willful control, even my finitude. Love is an admission of the power of powerlessness that cuts through the binary opposition of being and not being. Of course, there are other existential choices on display in *Hamlet:* Claudius's world of espionage and brutal political power, Polonius's foolish scholarship and mastery of cliché, Gertrude's conquest of personal satisfaction in the name of survival, Hamlet Junior's inhibited, suicidal, and chatty nihilism, even Hamlet Senior's spectral fiction of the existence of great men and kingly nobility. But we have tried to listen for something else in the distracted globe of *Hamlet,* words whispered in the wings, some other way of loving.

It is not without bucketfuls of shame that we write about *Hamlet.* The Shakespeare Industry is heavy with cultural gravitas, to say nothing of the mountainous literature that exists on *Hamlet* alone. It should take a scholar a lifetime to master it. We are but inauthentic amateurs, like some of those we have undertaken to work with in this book. We speak rashly of that which we know not (praised be rashness?). We write as outsiders, for shame, about Shakespeare, with the added shame of doing so as husband and wife with the implicit intent of writing about love. Perhaps we have completely betrayed ourselves. Perhaps this book will be the undoing of our marriage. Perhaps it is written in vain, for no one and for nothing. In this rash lovers' risk, this is essentially a book about nothing, for the love of nothing, for the nothing of love, for the love of *Hamlet*.

NOTES

INTRODUCTION

1. Sigmund Freud, *Notes upon a Case of Obsessional Neurosis* in *The Standard Edition of the Complete Psychological Works of Sigmund Freud,* ed. James Strachey, vol. 10 (London: Hogarth, 1909), 241.

2. Given his preference for the Folio text, Hibbard concurs with this cutting, claiming that Hamlet's final soliloquy, "for all its felicity of phrasing, is redundant. It tells us nothing we do not know already, except that the Prince has become unrealistic" (G. R. Hibbard, *Hamlet,* 109). For us, on the contrary, the poignancy and power of this last soliloquy reside in its lack of realism.

3. Harold Bloom, *Poem Unlimited* (New York: Riverhead, 2003), 230.

4. Ibid., 231.

5. Ibid., 147.

6. Herman Melville, *Pierre; or, The Ambiguities* (London: Penguin, 1996), 169.

7. Pierre gloomily goes on in his interpretation of *Hamlet,*
   If among the deeper significances of its pervading in-definiteness, which significances are wisely hidden from all but the rarest adepts, the pregnant tragedy of Hamlet convey any one particular moral at all fitted to the ordinary uses of man, it is this:— that all meditation is worthless, unless it prompt to action; that it is not for man to stand shilly-shallying amid the conflicting invasions of surrounding impulses; that in the earliest instant of conviction, the roused man must strike, and, if possible, with the precision and force of the lightning-bolt.

PART I

1. Carl Schmitt, *Hamlet or Hecuba: The Intrusion of Time into the Play,* trans. D. Pan and J. Rust (New York: Telos Press, 2009), 16.
2. Ibid., 18.
3. Ibid., 38.
4. Walter Benjamin, *The Origin of German Tragic Drama,* trans. J. Osborne (London: Verso, 1977), 65.
5. Schmitt, *Hamlet or Hecuba,* 44.
6. Ibid., 45.
7. Ibid.
8. Ibid., 49.
9. Benjamin, *Origin of German Tragic Drama,* 139–140.
10. Ibid.
11. Ibid., 142.
12. Ibid., 187.
13. Ibid., 139.
14. Ibid., 158.
15. It has to be asked: is not Benjamin subscribing to what we might call the exceptionalism of Shakespeare, common in German Romantic aesthetics and its epigones? It is, to say the least, unclear. Prima facie, it might be said that *Trauerspiel* is a dramatic form of baroque melancholia that is unable to attain any redemptive stance and therefore would appear to be inferior to Shakespeare's *Hamlet.* But if that is true, then this Christian interpretation of *Hamlet* would seem to betray the very historical analogy that Benjamin is trying to make between the baroque and the situation of Germany in particular and Europe in general in the 1920s. If the critical claim that Benjamin is obliquely trying to press is that his age is a neo-baroque culture of melancholy and sovereign indecision in a soulless world, then the redemption offered by *Hamlet* might be seen as delusional or, at worst, ideological. Certainly it is out of joint with the pile of corpses and the sound of ordnance that mark the end of the play. Indeed, going back to Benjamin's distinction between symbol and allegory, is not this Christian interpretation of *Hamlet* the quintessentially

symbolic gesture—namely finding the universal in the particular in a figure whose death would appear to be sacrificial in precisely the way Benjamin insists is only available in ancient tragedy?

16. Schmitt, *Hamlet or Hecuba,* 62.

17. Benjamin, *Origin of German Tragic Drama,* 64.

18. Ibid., 65.

19. Simon Williams, *Shakespeare on the German Stage, 1586–1941,* vol. 1 (Cambridge: Cambridge University Press, 1990). As Joseph Goebbels, who wrote his Ph.D. dissertation on nineteenth-century Romantic drama, noted in his diary in 1936 after seeing a production of *Hamlet* in Berlin, "What a genius Shakespeare is!"

20. Margreta de Grazia, *Hamlet Without Hamlet* (Cambridge: Cambridge University Press, 2007), chap. 6.

21. Benjamin, *Origin of German Tragic Drama,* 101.

22. G. W. F. Hegel, *Aesthetics: Lectures on Fine Art,* trans. T. M. Knox, vol. 2 (Oxford: Oxford University Press, 1975), 1,217–1,228.

23. Ibid., 1,231.

24. Ibid.

25. We are thinking of Marx's "Critique of Hegel's Doctrine of the State," from 1843, when Marx was in his midtwenties. See Karl Marx, *Early Writings,* ed. Lucio Colletti (Harmondsworth, UK: Penguin, 1975), 57–198.

26. Hegel, *Aesthetics,* 1,232.

27. Ibid., 1,231–1,232.

28. Ibid., 1,226.

PART II

1. See Shoshana Felman, *Literature and Psychoanalysis,* where she speaks about the problematic master-slave relationship between psychoanalysis and literature. Her book was a first effort by the American academy to find a new relationship between literature and psychoanalysis. The psychoanalyst shouldn't be in exclusive possession of some master key. She

claims that literary texts carry within themselves "an other scene" that provides a clue to their interpretation that can be read by all.

2. Sigmund Freud, "Psychopathic Characters on the Stage," in *The Standard Edition of the Complete Psychological Works of Sigmund Freud,* ed. James Strachey, vol. 7 (1953), 310.

3. Ernest Jones, *The Life and Work of Sigmund Freud,* vol. 3 (New York: Basic Books, 1981).

4. Ernest Jones claims that Freud's obsession with the historical figure of Shakespeare stemmed from his "family romance fantasy" and connects his preoccupation with the Earl of Oxford theory to his discomfort with the idea that Shakespeare was a man of lowly birth. This, he writes, follows Freud's preoccupation with the "real" Moses, who Freud thought was originally an Egyptian king rather than a Jew. While we are somewhat skeptical of Jones's claim—at least as an "explanation"—something important does linger in Freud's obsession with the *true* Shakespeare. In his self-analysis, Freud discovered a discomfort with his origins, in particular a lowering of status in his family due to a loss of wealth that forced the Freud family to move out of the country into the city. Freud often looked back on his early days in the country as a more noble and dignified life, full of pleasures that he felt he missed, including a young love. Bouts of depression were linked to this fantasy and feelings of being unable to rise up from his station. Would it not have been more interesting to tie Freud and Hamlet together through the notion of a family romance fantasy rather than speculate on either Freud's or Shakespeare's biography?

5. Lacan's important turn with respect to the place and function of literature in psychoanalysis is brilliantly elaborated by Jean-Michel Rabaté in his book *Jacques Lacan* (New York: Palgrave, 2001) to which we are enormously indebted. Rabaté writes:

> Not only does he [Lacan] show how much Freud and other practitioners rely on literary effects in many case studies, with all the subsequent narratological problems they entail, but he also follows Freud in the suggestion

that there is not opposition but complementarity between the literary domain and "real cases.". . . . He [Lacan] reads them in order to understand something about human nature, which may sound grandiose but it should not be forgotten that his approach is founded on what he constantly calls the "experience" of psychoanalysis . . . this experience is an experience of language as living speech, a fundamental factor that Lacan puts to the fore. . . . This is why Lacan's lifelong confrontation with literature has always hinged on the basic and almost naïve questions, such as, why do we write? Why do we read? What touches us in this apparently simple process? . . . One consequence of these fundamental questions is that they imply a radical critique of everything that has been produced under the name of applied psychoanalysis or psychoanalytical criticism. As he states in texts devoted to single authors such as Duras and Joyce, Lacan refuses to psychoanalyse either the author or the works. This would be too easy and would miss the mark [2–3].

6. Throughout this chapter, we will refer to both the unpublished translation of a transcription of Lacan's seminar "Desire and Its Interpretation" by Cormac Gallagher and an edited selection from the seminar published in *Yale French Studies*. There are significant differences between the two versions, and both are used to elucidate Lacan's treatment of the play.

7. Seminar 6 is positioned midway between Lacan's 1957–58 seminar, "The Formations of the Unconscious," and his 1959–60 seminar 7, "The Ethics of Psychoanalysis," which contains his famous—indeed infamous—interpretation of *Antigone*.

8. The problem of Freud's abandonment of the seduction theory continues to haunt psychoanalysis and psychology. Many see the move as crucial for developing a more complex model of the psyche. Others see this move as a disavowal of real trauma in children and adults from sexual abuse to other forms of abuse that are experienced traumatically. The arguments here can be seen to circle around whether Freud's theory is a theory of conflict or a theory of deficit, meaning humans are conflicted by sexuality that produces symptoms (and this would be the case for everyone and is only exacerbated by trauma) or

real trauma causes a deficit in one's mental development, and there are others who are spared this fate. See Leonard Shengold, *Soul Murder: The Effects of Childhood Abuse and Deprivation* (New York: Ballantine Books, 1991).

9. See Henriette Michaud's *Les revenants de la mémoire: Freud et Shakespeare* (Presses Universitaires de France, 2011).

10. Sigmund Freud, *The Interpretation of Dreams* in *The Standard Edition of the Complete Psychological Works of Sigmund Freud,* ed. James Strachey, vol. 4 (London: Hogarth, 1900), 262–263.

11. Ibid., 264.

12. Ibid., 441.

13. Ernest Jones, *The Life and Work of Sigmund Freud,* vol. 2 (New York: Basic Books, 1981), 421.

14. Sigmund Freud, "On Narcissism: An Introduction" in *The Standard Edition of the Complete Psychological Works of Sigmund Freud,* ed. James Strachey, vol. 14 (London: Hogarth, 1914), 98.

15. Sigmund Freud, "Mourning and Melancholia," in *The Standard Edition of the Complete Psychological Works of Sigmund Freud,* ed. James Strachey, vol. 14 (London: Hogarth, 1917), 247.

16. Ibid., 246–247.

17. Jacques Lacan et al., "Desire and the Interpretation of Desire in *Hamlet,*" trans. James Hubert, *Yale French Studies* 55/56 (1977), 46.

18. The footnote in the *Yale French Studies* edition to the reference to *schöne Seele,* made famous by Goethe's *Wilhelm Meister,* is important to underline, for it is a concept that Lacan refers to regularly and that remains unexplained in the quotation:

> Allusion to Hegel's dialectic of the withdrawn, and contemplative "beautiful soul". . . generally considered itself an allusion in turn to a variety of eighteenth and early nineteenth-century writers, primarily in Germany. In several other contexts, Lacan links this dialectic to others in the *Phenomenology* ("master-slave," "law of the heart") and stresses that the beautiful soul denounces the perceived disorder of the world around him without recognizing that this disorder is a reflection of his own inner

state. See *Écrits* [trans. Bruce Fink (New York: Norton, 2007)], pp. 171–73, 281, 292, 415.

19. Lacan, "Desire and the Interpretation of Desire in *Hamlet*," 45.

20. Jacques Lacan, "Seminar VI: Desire and Its Interpretation," unpublished, trans. Cormac Gallagher (1958–59), 177.

21. Lacan, "Desire and the Interpretation of Desire in Hamlet," 18–19. In Harold Bloom's essay on *Hamlet* he quotes W. H. Auden's interpretation as "the oddest opinion in the *Hamlet* criticism of our time." It is very close to Lacan's interpretation, as the following quotation reveals:

> Hamlet lacks faith in God and in himself. Consequently he must define his existence in terms of others, e.g., I am the man whose mother married his uncle who murdered his father. He would like to become what the Greek tragic hero is, a creature of situation. Hence his inability to act, for he can only "act," i.e., play at possibilities.

For Auden, the contrast should be between Don Quixote and Hamlet: the one who acts and the one who "acts."

22. Lacan, "Seminar VI: Desire and Its Interpretation," 221.

23. Ibid., 178.

24. Stuart Schneiderman, *Jacques Lacan: The Death of an Intellectual Hero* (Cambridge, MA: Harvard University Press, 1983), 153–154.

25. See Jacques Derrida, *Chaque fois unique, la fin du monde,* ed. Pascale-Anne Brault and Michael Naas (Paris: Galilée, 2003).

26. Lacan, "Seminar VI: Desire and Its Interpretation," 230.

27. Ibid.

28. Jacques Lacan, *Écrits,* trans. Bruce Fink (New York: Norton, 2006), 80.

29. Lacan, after taking Bataille's wife, Sylvie, and marrying her, praised Bataille as the consummate male hysteric, a mystic, and clearly also a fierce rival of Lacan. See Roudinesco's biography *Jacques Lacan.*

30. Georges Bataille, *Visions of Excess: Selected Writings, 1927–1935,* trans. Allan Stoekl (Minneapolis: University of Minnesota Press, 1985), 12–13.

31. We owe a "truepenny" debt here to Tom McCarthy for his brilliant insights into Shakespeare's sonnets.

32. Lacan, "Seminar VI: Desire and Its Interpretation," 233.
33. Ibid., 168.
34. Ibid., 229.
35. Ibid., 194.
36. Ibid., 195.
37. The use of *dénégation* here suggests that "Hamlet's hostile references to Claudius can be interpreted as indications of repressed admiration" (Lacan, "Desire and the Interpretation of Desire," *Yale French Studies,* 50), insofar as the force of negation in his insults is working hard to struggle against its opposite. The splitting of the object, idealized and denigrated, is linked by psychoanalysis to its retaining omnipotence or phallic value in the unconscious.
38. Lacan, "Desire and the Interpretation of Desire in *Hamlet,*" 50.
39. Lacan, "Seminar VI: Desire and Its Interpretation," 183–184.
40. Ibid., 196.
41. Ibid., 184.
42. Ibid., 247.
43. Lacan, *Écrits,* 81.

PART III

1. Friedrich Nietzsche, *The Birth of Tragedy and the Case of Wagner,* trans. W. Kaufmann (New York: Vintage, 1967), 19.
2. Friedrich Nietzsche, *Ecce Homo,* trans. D. Large, (Oxford: Oxford University Press, 2007), 78.
3. *Double Take,* directed by Johan Grimonprez and Tom McCarthy (2009; Kino International, 2010), DVD.
4. Nietzsche, *Birth of Tragedy,* 82.
5. Ibid., 80.
6. Ibid., 83–84.
7. Ibid., 74.
8. Ibid., 65.
9. Ibid., 37.
10. Nietzsche, *Ecce Homo,* 81.
11. Nietzsche, *Birth of Tragedy,* 59–60.
12. That Nietzsche is aware of the stakes of this claim can be seen

from his discussion of Schopenhauer in the 1886 preface, where he asks, "What, after all, did Schopenhauer think of tragedy?" To which he replies with a quotation from *The World as Will and Representation:* "It leads to resignation"(Nietzsche, *Birth of Tragedy,* 24).

13. This experience of desire is wonderfully described by Augustine in book 10 of *Confessions,* where he agonizes about the virtue involved in the sensual pleasure of religious music. On the question that Augustine poses to God, he writes:

> But do you, O Lord my God, graciously hear me, and turn your gaze upon me, and see me, and have mercy upon me, and heal me. For in your sight I have become a question to myself and that is my languor [*mihi quaestio factus sum et ipse est languor meus*].

In Augustine, languor is the question that one becomes for oneself in relation to the distant, watching Jansenist God who may heal and have mercy upon us but whom we cannot know and whose grace cannot be guaranteed. The questions that Augustine poses to God make him a question to himself, and this induces the experience of languor, where time itself assumes a languid quality: distending, stretching out, procrastinating.

14. There is an interesting and growing literature on disgust, which perhaps begins with Aurel Kolnai's two fascinating phenomenological papers on disgust—bookends to his philosophical career—the first written in 1927 and the second from 1969 to 1970. Kolnai itemizes the traits of the "materially disgusting" in phenomena like putrefaction, excrement, bodily secretion, dirt, the swarming of insects, decaying food, stinking feces, and so on.

15. Friedrich Nietzsche, *The Gay Science,* trans. W. Kaufmann (New York: Vintage, 1974), 98.

16. Nietzsche, *Ecce Homo,* 59.

17. We'd like to thank Keith Ansell-Pearson for his invaluable help on Nietzsche's understanding of *Hamlet.*

18. Nietzsche, *Ecce Homo,* 93.

19. Ibid., 88.

20. Ibid., 10.

21. Indeed, there is an odd homonymic and crazily alliterative

echo of "machine" in Hamlet's "Marry, this is miching mallecho. It means mischief."

22. Edward Payson Vining, *The Mystery of Hamlet* (Philadelphia: J. B. Lippincott: 1881), 46.

23. Ibid., 59.

CONCLUSION

1. There are nine references to shame in the play. Polonius says to Laertes:

> *Yet here, Laertes! aboard, aboard, for shame!*
> *The wind sits in the shoulder of your sail,*
> *And you are stay'd for.*

The ghost says,

> *O wicked wit and gifts, that have the power*
> *So to seduce!—won to his shameful lust*
> *The will of my most seeming-virtuous queen:*
> *O Hamlet, what a falling-off was there!*

Hamlet says to Ophelia about the dumb show: "Ay, or any show that you'll show him: be not you ashamed to show, he'll not shame to tell you what it means." Hamlet says to his mother: "O shame! Where is thy blush?" and "proclaim no shame / When the compulsive ardor gives the charge." Hamlet says to himself: "And let all sleep? While, to my shame, I see / The imminent death of twenty thousand men." Ophelia sings:

> *By Gis and by Saint Charity*
> *Alack, and fie for shame!*
> *Young men will do't, if they come to't;*
> *By cock, they are to blame.*

Laertes says at Ophelia's funeral: "Let shame say what it will: when these are gone / The woman will be out." Hamlet says to Osric: "I will win for him an I can; if not, I will gain nothing but my shame and the odd hits."

BIBLIOGRAPHY

EDITIONS OF *HAMLET* USED IN THE WRITING OF THIS BOOK

Dolven, Jeff, ed. 2007. *Hamlet,* New York: Barnes & Noble.

Hibbard, G. R., ed. 1987. *Hamlet.* Oxford: Oxford University Press.

Jenkins, Harold, ed. 1982. *Hamlet.* Arden Shakespeare, 2nd series. London: Arden Shakespeare.

Raffel, Burton, introduction. 2003. *Hamlet.* Fully annotated with an essay by Harold Bloom. New Haven, CT: Yale University Press.

Thompson, Ann, and Neil Taylor, eds. 2006. Arden Shakespeare, 3rd series. London: Arden Shakespeare.

———. 2006. *Hamlet: The Texts of 1603 and 1623.* Arden Shakespeare, 3rd series. London: Arden Shakespeare.

OTHER WORKS

Adorno, Theodor. 1974. *Minima Moralia.* Translated by E. F. N. Jephcott. London: Verso.

———. 2006. *History and Freedom.* Translated by Rodney Livingstone. Cambridge: Polity.

Bataille, Georges. 1985. *Visions of Excess: Selected Writings, 1927–1935.* Translated by Allan Stoekl. Minneapolis: University of Minnesota Press.

———. 1989. *The Accursed Share.* Vols. 2 and 3. Translated by Robert Hurley. New York: Zone Books.

Benjamin, Walter. 1977. *The Origin of German Tragic Drama.* Translated by J. Osborne. London: Verso.

Bloom, Harold. 2003. *Poem Unlimited.* New York: Riverhead.

Butler, Judith. 2010. *Frames of War.* London and New York: Verso.

Cavarero, Adriana. 2002. *Stately Bodies: Literature, Philosophy, and the Question of Gender,* Translated by R. De Lucca and Deanna Shemek. Ann Arbor: University of Michigan Press.

Cavell, Stanley. 2003. "Hamlet's Burden of Proof." In *Disowning Knowledge: In Seven Plays of Shakespeare.* Cambridge: Cambridge University Press.

Cobain, Kurt. 2002. *Journals.* New York: Riverhead Books.

Coleridge, Samuel Taylor. 1976. *Treatise on Method.* London: Norwood.

———. 1987. "1811–12 Lectures on Shakespeare and Milton." In *Lectures on Literature, 1808–19,* edited by R. A. Foakes. London: Routledge.

Cross, Charles R. 2001. *Heavier Than Heaven: A Biography of Kurt Cobain.* New York: Hyperion.

De Grazia, Margreta. 2007. Hamlet *Without Hamlet.* Cambridge: Cambridge University Press.

Derrida, Jacques. 1994. *Specters of Marx.* Translated by Peggy Kamuf. London: Routledge.

———. 2003. *Chaque fois unique, la fin du monde,* edited by Pascale-Anne Brault and Michael Naas. Paris: Galilée.

Eliot, T. S. 1997. "Hamlet and His Problems." In *The Sacred Wood.* London: Faber.

Felman, Shoshana. 1977. *Literature and Psychoanalysis: The Question of Reading: Otherwise.* Baltimore and London: Johns Hopkins University Press.

Freud, Sigmund. 1900. *The Interpretation of Dreams.* Volumes 4 and 5 of *The Standard Edition of the Complete Psychological Works of Sigmund Freud,* edited by James Strachey. London: Hogarth.

———. 1909. *Notes upon a Case of Obsessional Neurosis.* Vol. 10 of *The Standard Edition of the Complete Psychological Works of Sigmund Freud,* edited by James Strachey. London: Hogarth.

———. 1910. "A Special Type of Object-Choice Made by Men." In vol. 1 of *Contributions to the Psychology of Love.* Vol. 11 of *The Standard Edition of the Complete Psychological Works of Sigmund Freud,* edited by James Strachey. London: Hogarth.

————. 1911. *Psycho-Analytic Notes on an Autobiographical Account of a Case of Paranoia (Dementia Paranoides)*. Vol. 12 of *The Standard Edition of the Complete Psychological Works of Sigmund Freud*, edited by James Strachey. London: Hogarth.

————. 1912. "On the Universal Tendency to Debasement in the Sphere of Love." In vol. 2 of *Contributions to the Psychology of Love*. Vol. 11 of *The Standard Edition of the Complete Psychological Works of Sigmund Freud*, edited by James Strachey. London: Hogarth.

————. 1913. *Totem and Taboo*. Vol. 13 of *The Standard Edition of the Complete Psychological Works of Sigmund Freud*, edited by James Strachey. London: Hogarth.

————. 1914. "On Narcissism: An Introduction." Vol. 14 of *The Standard Edition of the Complete Psychological Works of Sigmund Freud*, edited by James Strachey. London: Hogarth.

————. 1917. "Mourning and Melancholia." In vol. 14 of *The Standard Edition of the Complete Psychological Works of Sigmund Freud*, edited by James Strachey. London: Hogarth.

————. 1919. "The Uncanny." In vol. 17 of *The Standard Edition of the Complete Psychological Works of Sigmund Freud*, edited by James Strachey. London: Hogarth.

————. 1921. *Group Psychology and the Analysis of the Ego*. Vol. 18 of *The Standard Edition of the Complete Psychological Works of Sigmund Freud*, edited by James Strachey. London: Hogarth.

————. 1922. "Some Neurotic Mechanisms in Jealousy, Paranoia and Homosexuality." In vol. 18 of *The Standard Edition of the Complete Psychological Works of Sigmund Freud*, edited by James Strachey. London: Hogarth.

————. 1924. "The Dissolution of the Oedipus Complex." In vol. 19 of *The Standard Edition of the Complete Psychological Works of Sigmund Freud*, edited by James Strachey. London: Hogarth.

————. 1930. *Civilization and Its Discontents*. Vol. 21 of *The Standard Edition of the Complete Psychological Works of Sigmund Freud*, edited by James Strachey. London: Hogarth.

————. 1930. "The Goethe Prize: Address Delivered in the Goethe

House at Frankfurt." In vol. 21 of *The Standard Edition of the Complete Psychological Works of Sigmund Freud,* edited by James Strachey. London: Hogarth.

———. 1939. *Moses and Monotheism: Three Essays.* Vol. 23 of *The Standard Edition of the Complete Psychological Works of Sigmund Freud,* edited by James Strachey. London: Hogarth.

———. 1953. "Psychopathic Characters on the Stage." In vol. 7 of *The Standard Edition of the Complete Psychological Works of Sigmund Freud,* edited by James Strachey. London: Hogarth.

———. 1974. *The Standard Edition of the Complete Psychological Works of Sigmund Freud.* Edited by James Strachey. 24 vols. London: Hogarth.

———. 1985. *The Complete Letters of Sigmund Freud to Wilhelm Fliess, 1887–1904.* Cambridge, MA, and London: Harvard University Press.

Frye, Northrop. 1986. *On Shakespeare.* Edited by Robert Sandler. New Haven, CT: Yale University Press.

Goethe, J. W. von. 1989. *Wilhelm Meister's Apprenticeship.* Translated by Eric A. Blackall. New York: Suhrkamp.

Green, André. 1982. *Hamlet et Hamlet.* Paris: Balland.

Greenblatt, Stephen. 2001. *Hamlet in Purgatory.* Princeton, NJ: Princeton University Press.

Grimonprez, Johan. 2007. *Looking for Alfred.* London: Film and Video Umbrella.

Haverkamp, Anselm. 2010. *Shakespearean Genealogies of Power.* London: Routledge.

Hegel, G. W. F. 1975. *Aesthetics: Lectures on Fine Art.* Vol 2. Translated by T. M. Knox. Oxford: Oxford University Press.

———. 1975. *On Natural Law.* Translated by T. M. Knox. Philadelphia: University of Pennsylvania Press.

———. 1977. *Phenomenology of Spirit.* Translated by A. V. Miller. Oxford: Oxford University Press.

———. 2008. *Philosophy of Right.* Translated by T. M. Knox. Oxford: Oxford University Press.

Honig, Bonnie. 2010. "Antigone's Two Laws: Greek Tragedy and the Politics of Humanism." *New Literary History* 41, no. 1: 1–33.

Jones, Ernest. 1976. *Hamlet and Oedipus.* New York: Norton.

————. 1981. *The Life and Work of Sigmund Freud.* Vols. 1–3. New York: Basic Books.

Joyce, James. 1967. *Ulysses.* London: Bodley Head.

Kearney, Richard. 2004. "Kierkegaard on Hamlet: Between Art and Religion." In *The New Kierkegaard.* Edited by Elsebet Jegstrup. Bloomington and Indianapolis, IN: Indiana University Press.

Kierkegaard, Søren. 1988. *Stages on Life's Way.* Edited and translated by Howard V. Hong and Edna H. Hong. Princeton, NJ: Princeton University Press.

Kolnai, Aurel. 2004. *On Disgust.* Chicago and La Salle, IL: Open Court.

Kottman, Paul. 2009. *Tragic Conditions in Shakespeare.* Baltimore: Johns Hopkins University Press.

Lacan, Jacques. 1958–59. "Seminar VI: Desire and Its Interpretation." Translated by Cormac Gallagher. Unpublished.

————. 1992. *Seminar VII: The Ethics of Psychoanalysis.* Translated by D. Porter. New York: Norton.

————. 1998. *Les Formations de l'Inconscient.* Paris: Seuil.

————. 1998. *Seminar XI: The Four Fundamental Concepts of Psychoanalysis.* Translated by Alan Sheridan. New York: Norton.

————. 2007. *Écrits.* Translated by Bruce Fink. New York: Norton.

Lacan, Jacques, et al. 1977. "Desire and the Interpretation of Desire in *Hamlet.*" *Yale French Studies* 55/56, 11–52.

Marx, Karl. 1975. *Early Writings.* Edited by L. Colletti. Harmondsworth, UK: Penguin.

Melville, Herman. 1996. *Pierre; or, The Ambiguities.* London: Penguin.

Menke, Christoph. 2009. "Tragedy and Skepticism: On *Hamlet.*" In *Tragic Play.* New York: Columbia University Press.

Michaud, Henriette. 2011. *Les revenants de la mémoire: Freud et Shakespeare.* Paris: Presses Universitaires de France.

Müller, Heiner. 1984. *Hamletmachine and Other Texts for the Stage.* Edited by Carl Weber. New York: Performing Arts Journal Publications.

————. 2012. *After Shakespeare.* Translated by Carl Weber and Paul David Young. New York: Performing Arts Journal Publications.

Nietzsche, Friedrich. 1967. *The Birth of Tragedy and the Case of Wagner.* Translated by W. Kaufmann. New York: Vintage.

———. 1974. *The Gay Science.* Translated by W. Kaufmann. New York: Vintage.

———. 2007. *Ecce Homo.* Translated by D. Large. Oxford: Oxford University Press.

Rabaté, Jean-Michel. 2001. *Jacques Lacan.* New York: Palgrave.

Rieff, Philip. 1959. *Freud: The Mind of the Moralist.* Chicago: University of Chicago Press.

Roudinesco, Élisabeth. 1997. *Jacques Lacan.* Translated by Barbara Bray. New York: Columbia University Press.

Santner, Eric. 2010. *The Royal Remains.* Chicago: University of Chicago Press.

Schmitt, Carl. 1985. *Political Theology: Four Chapters on the Concept of Sovereignty.* Translated by G. Schwab. Chicago: University of Chicago Press.

———. 2009. *Hamlet or Hecuba: The Intrusion of Time into the Play.* Translated by D. Pan and J. Rust. New York: Telos Press.

———. 2010. "Foreword to the German Edition of Lilian Winstanley's *Hamlet and the Scottish Succession.*" *Telos* 153 (Winter 2010) 164–77.

Schneiderman, Stuart. 1983. *Jacques Lacan: The Death of an Intellectual Hero.* Cambridge, MA: Harvard University Press.

Vernant, Jean-Pierre, and Pierre Vidal-Naquet. 1988. *Myth and Tragedy in Ancient Greece.* Translated by J. Lloyd. New York: Zone Books.

Vining, Edward Payson. 1881. *The Mystery of Hamlet.* Philadelphia: J. B. Lippincott.

Williams, Bernard. 1993. *Shame and Necessity.* Berkeley and Los Angeles: University of California Press.

Williams, Raymond. 1966. *Modern Tragedy.* Stanford: Stanford University Press.

———. 2007. "Afterword to *Modern Tragedy.*" In *Politics of Modernism.* London: Verso.

Williams, Simon. 1990. *1586–1914.* Vol. 1 of *Shakespeare on the German Stage.* Cambridge: Cambridge University Press.

Woolf, Virginia. 2008. "On Being Ill." In *Selected Essays,* edited by D. Bradshaw. Oxford: Oxford University Press.

DVDS

Branagh, Kenneth. 1996 (DVD 2007). *William Shakespeare's Hamlet.* Directed by Kenneth Branagh. Warner Brothers.

Burton, Richard. 1964 (DVD 1999). *Hamlet.* Directed by John Gielgud. Image Entertainment.

Clark, Christopher. 1995. *X Hamlet.* Directed by Luca Damiano. Tip Top Entertainment.

Gibson, Mel. 1990 (DVD 2004). *Hamlet.* Directed by Franco Zeffirelli. Warner Home Video.

Grimonprez, Johan. 2009 (DVD 2010). *Double Take.* Directed by Johan Grimonprez and Tom McCarthy. Kino International.

Hawke, Ethan. 2003. *Hamlet.* Directed by Michael Almereyda. Lionsgate.

Olivier, Laurence. 1948 (DVD 2000). *Hamlet.* Directed by Laurence Olivier. Criterion.

Tennant, David. 2009 (DVD 2010). The Royal Shakespeare Company Production of *Hamlet.* Directed by Gregory Doran. BBC Worldwide.

Smoktunovsky, Innokenti. 1964. (DVD 2006). *Hamlet.* Directed by Grigori Kozintsev. Russian Cinema Council.

Williamson, Nicol. 1969 (DVD 2012). *Hamlet.* Directed by Tony Richardson. Columbia Pictures.

INDEX

Gorgiastic paradox, 15–17, 18–19,
    22, 27, 45, 191, 231
Greenblatt, Stephen, 66
*Group Psychology and the Analysis
    of the Ego* (Freud), 144, 191
Guildenstern, 9, 19, 29–31, 37, 48,
    75, 132, 224–5
guilt, 230

Hamlet:
    after death, 225–7
    alleged incestuous feelings of,
        61, 87, 168–9
    as allegedly changed after return
        from England, 36–8, 142
    as Christ and Adam, 38
    Claudius insulted by, 174, 246
    Claudius's criticism of,
        79–80, 99
    critics' seeing selves in, 90
    on defying augury, 11–12, 36,
        67, 70
    depression of, 5, 13, 37, 65, 70,
        123, 126, 168, 204
    distaste for sexuality of, 108
    dying wish of, 66–7, 134
    estrangement of, 136
    father idealized by, 86
    Fortinbras praised in soliloquy
        of, 31–3
    Freud's identification with, 110,
        112
    Gertrude and Claudius merged
        in imagination of, 172
    "Get thee to a nunnery" speech
        of, 160–1, 198–9
    ghost doubted by, 22–3, 25

    as hysteric, 102, 135
    identified with Laertes, 138–40,
        141–6, 147, 188, 224
    inauthenticity of, 223
    indecisiveness of, 5–7, 8–9,
        11–12, 13, 33, 42–5, 85, 98,
        103–4, 108–9, 167, 170–1, 211
    Laertes as rival of, 33–4
    Laertes's duel with, 35–6, 52,
        137, 142, 224
    Laertes's wrestling with, 37, 130,
        141, 145
    on language, 21–2
    love for Ophelia and, 23–4, 34,
        51, 54, 116, 124–5, 152, 153,
        181, 233
    on marriage, 3
    misanthropy of, 203, 204, 212
    mood swings of, 13, 37, 51, 109,
        181, 223–4
    mourning by, 162–3, 168
    mourning denied to, 119–21
    Müller's version of, 211–15
    murder of Claudius passed up
        by, 89
    nihilism, 26–38, 131
    as nothing, 28
    obscenities to Ophelia from,
        27–8
    Oedipus and, 5, 43, 96, 98, 99,
        100, 102–4, 106, 107–10, 111,
        126–7, 164, 167–8, 170, 174
    on original sin, 80–1
    overthinking by, 5–7, 8–9, 11, 33,
        43, 65, 69, 212
    as political threat to Claudius,
        50, 51, 53–4
    Polonius killed by, 9, 29, 48, 77,
        112, 139–40, 171–2, 178

Printed in the United States
by Baker & Taylor Publisher Services